AWAKEN TO
GOOD MOURNING

by Mark E. Hundley

Dany,

Please accept this as an expression of my sympathy. I can't imagine the loss you are experiencing.

Respectfully,
Vanessa

No part of this book may be reproduced or transmitted in any form, or by any means, without permission in writing from the Publisher.

Published by:
Awaken Publications
P.O. Box 940727
Plano, Texas, 75094

This publication is not designed to present a completely comprehensive overview of the subject matter. It represents the findings of one individual, and is not intended as a substitute for professional, legal or medical advice. If expert assistance is required, the services of a competent professional should be sought.

This book is available at special discounts for bulk purchases by groups, organizations and individuals. For details, contact the Publisher at (214) 578-6018.

Edited by Sally Bradford
Cover and Book Design by Dusty Crocker
PARTNERS/creative (817) 469-9440

ISBN 0-9640916-0-7
Previously ISBN 0-9637563-0-3

TABLE OF CONTENTS

PREFACE

*T*his book is born from my own personal experience with death, mourning and recovery. I, like so many others in our society, was not prepared to face the excruciating pain associated with the death of a loved one when my wife, Christy, was killed in an automobile accident on January 24, 1989. I suddenly found myself as the single father of a seven-year-old daughter. I was numb, angry, confused, frightened and searching — searching for some kind of guidance and support to help me get through the tasks which lay ahead of me. Fortunately, because of my background in counseling and religion, I had many friends and colleagues on which to call for help and support. I was fortunate to know where to look to get the assistance I so desperately needed at that time, yet I was aware of how much more difficult it would have been for me and my daughter if I had not known where to find that help.

As I worked through my grief, I learned many practical principles and discovered some very helpful resources around which I began to rebuild my life. I further became convinced that these principles and resources needed to be shared with other individuals and families facing the devastation of the death of a loved one. I do not claim that this volume contains all that is necessary for individuals and families to successfully rebuild in the aftermath of the death of a loved one, but it does contain the gleanings from my own pilgrimage. In effect, I present to you a way of approaching the grief process — a way that has worked for me that may also provide you some comfort and assistance. It is my hope and prayer that you will find the information contained in these pages useful as you work through your own grief.

ACKNOWLEDGEMENTS

I owe a great deal of gratitude to many people who have supported me, listened to me, encouraged me and loved me through my journey. To Roy Austin, Ph.D., my friend and therapist who has been a constant encouragement both personally and professionally, I express my deepest thanks. I thank my daughter, Kacie, who has served as a model of courage and determination — she has taught me what a child's view of grief and mourning is all about. I am indebted to Joyce and Keith Laseter, my late wife Christy's parents, who have been a consistent support and who have taught me about the grief of parents. I thank my mother and stepfather, Barbara and Owen Oslin, and my father and stepmother, Ed and Jane Hundley, who have loved me and prayed for me. I also thank my sister and brother-in-law, Majetta and David Green, for their heartfelt love and support. I thank the countless other friends and family members — all of whom alone could fill the pages of a single volume — for their selfless giving during my ordeal. While nothing can ever change my feelings or take Christy's place in my life, I have been comforted by these friends and loved ones during my rebuilding. I have learned that it is all right to save a place in my heart for Christy's memory while moving on to share my life with others. This process ultimately led me into a friendship which developed into a nurturing, loving new marriage in March of 1991. It is with this in mind that I also thank my wife, best friend and co-worker, Vanessa Hay, for her support, encouragement and love. This relationship is my primary source of strength as I seek to assist grieving individuals and families with the task of learning what Good Mourning can be.

INTRODUCTION

About this Book

This book is divided into four major sections — three describing the process of mourning and one offering the encouragement to get you on the path to your own Good Mourning. The appendix section is divided into four parts, each offering its own useful resources to help guide you in your grief work.

It is my belief that the process of mourning is best described in terms of phases rather than stages. The concept of stages tends to cause people to think in terms of a linear and sequential movement through the process. This line of thinking encourages individuals to believe that as one goes through a particular stage, he or she will not experience the emotions connected with that stage again. Viewing the process of mourning in phases, on the other hand, allows for the identification of various emotions connected with grief work and, at the same time, provides a structure in which the overlapping and intertwining of emotions may occur.

I have chosen to identify the mourning process as occurring in three phases: Early Mourning — The Loss Event, Mid Mourning — The Transition, and Late Mourning — The Continuation. Each section contains discussions of the characteristics, the challenges and the choices unique to each phase.

Later in this introduction is a discussion of the book's title, what it means and how it differs from common methods of "bad" mourning. The final chapter is intended to help you on your way to a more positive mourning experience.

I hope, as you read this book, that you will realize it can be used again and again while you work through your loss. Allow yourself to read, reflect, review and re-read the information contained here many times — and share it with friends and family members.

Defining Terms

In this book, you will notice references to the terms "grief work" and the "grief process," or mourning process. These terms are similar, yet refer to two distinct aspects of what you are facing. The grief, or mourning, process refers to the actual "process" through which you go as you deal with your loss. It is the description of emotions, characteristics, challenges, choices and response patterns common to individuals grieving the loss of loved ones. The process may be observed, defined, charted and conceptualized to help clarify what you may expect to face as you deal with loss.

The term "grief work," on the other hand, refers to the actual steps you take to grieve your loss. Grief work focuses on activities in which you will engage in an effort to integrate this loss into the framework of your life as you continue living. Activities such as talking, writing, reading, support group participation and therapy are all examples of "grief work." It is the personal, unique approach you choose to take to work on your issues as you move through the grief process.

Why 'Good' Mourning?

The title of this book, "Awaken to Good Mourning," is my attempt to share the idea that the process of mourning the loss of your loved one can be healthy, positive and healing. I believe that a vast number of people do not experience healing from the pain of loss and, therefore, never experience the healthy, positive aspects of this process. This negative experience may be referred to as "bad mourning."

Bad mourning experiences tend to bring about compounded and complicated grief and can cause unresolved losses to build up in your life. Societal injunctions, family rules and personal belief systems tend to reinforce bad mourning. Bad mourning experiences often center around denial of feelings, repression of emotions and thoughts related to the pain of loss, over-involvement in activities such as work, social causes and exercise in order to medicate the feelings of pain and loneliness, and the rule that talking about your pain is inappropriate. My experience with people verifies that many individuals experience bad mourning as they seek to cope with loss and death. Bad mourning not only keeps you from healing and recovering, it can also have long-term negative effects on other aspects of your life as well.

"Good mourning," on the other hand, asserts that you can experience healing and emerge in a healthy way from the pain of loss. Good mourning is not a magical short cut through the grief process. It is not an easy way out of your pain. Rather, it is the process of honestly facing the reality of your loss, coming to terms with its impact on your life, learning to access all available resources for your recovery and continuing to live productively following this process.

The concept of good mourning may run contrary to the norm in your life where loss is involved. For this reason, I insist that you may, possibly for the first time, find yourself awakening to the idea that mourning your loss can, indeed, be a good, healthy, healing experience. You may find yourself entering into a new way of thinking, feeling and acting. The possibility of good mourning experiences can shed a new light on the necessary tasks of mourning which lie ahead of you.

Obviously, the tasks of good mourning are not easily faced. This book will seek to address each task by providing practical, understandable and useful information and resources — the end result being a guide to which you may turn again and again as you progress through your "grief work."

Identifying 'Bad' Mourning

In reading this book, you should keep in mind the various methods of bad mourning. Each coping mechanism, in itself, is perfectly normal and may be experienced in your early grief. However, it is when these responses to your loss continue -- or keep you from picking up the pieces and moving on with your life -- that they can become dangerous.

As you approach the task of mourning, consider ways to make your experience more healthy. Reflect on these warning signs of bad mourning and look for ways to avoid their traps as you move on to your personal Good Mourning. I urge you to refer to this section occasionally as a way of keeping yourself on the positive track to recovery.

1. Denial/Projection — People who use denial or projection as a way of coping may say things like: "These things happen to others, not to me!" "I don't have to deal with this." "If I ignore this, it will go away." If you choose to use this style of coping with loss, you may run the risk of living in a "created reality" or a "fantasy world" in which the rules of the game may be changed any time a threat to this reality is perceived. This approach allows you to keep running from the circumstances. Eventually, the reality of the situation will break through and you may be faced with an extremely difficult job of confronting the loss. This could unnecessarily compound and complicate your mourning efforts.

2. Fear/Pessimism — In your grief, you might hear yourself saying: "I hope that these things (death, sickness, loneliness, etc.) will not happen to me, but I am afraid they will." "The world is a dangerous place, therefore, I must be careful and not take risks." If you choose to use this system as a pattern in facing grief, you may end up developing a type of emotional, spiritual and relational paralysis. Fear and pessimism can cause you to choose to stay within the confines of the familiar and comfortable, even when those confines are harmful to your emotional well-being.

3. Trade-off/Bargaining — Have you ever said something like: "If I am good (pray, give money, help the poor, etc.), then these things will not happen to me!" "I will make a deal with God (the Universe, the Stars, the cards, etc.), and everything will be okay!" Consistent use of this system can lead to magical thinking. If you are not careful, you could be duped into believing that certain activities, promises or associations will keep tragedy, pain and grief away, or will provide you with security, health and wealth. Obviously, this is not the case. This system can serve to set you up for huge disappointments when the guarantee or deal does not work out as promised. It may force you to seek another formula, deal or guru from which to receive more false security. You may find yourself hopping from one promise to another without experiencing any real relief in your mourning.

4. Fatalism/Hopelessness — Sometimes people say: "Bad things are going to happen to me anyway, so why fight them?" "Nothing ever goes my way — I am just doomed to live this way." If you employ this system fairly regularly, you may discover that depression is a constant companion. I am not talking about acute or situational depression associated with grieving the loss of a loved one, which is a common experience of the grieving process. The depression which can result from this type of unhealthy system is the kind which may lead to addictive activities and behaviors intended to medicate the feelings of loneliness and helplessness associated with loss. Often, drug and alcohol abuse emerge from this type of attitude, which only further reinforce the futility of life, thus inhibiting your ability to recover and integrate loss.

5. False Guilt — Grieving individuals often say: "What did I do to cause this to happen?" "If only I would have said (done, known, heard, etc.) something else, this would not have happened." "It's all my fault!" If you consistently operate within this system, you run the risk of developing a delusion of reference — where everything that happens somehow relates to something you either did or did not do. You may truly feel responsible for things over which you have had no control at all. This is false guilt! The

comical side of this system is something in which we have all found ourselves at one time or another. For instance, how many times have you said, "Well, I washed my car so it is bound to rain!" — as if there were a rain cloud floating around the sky looking specifically for your car! That's pretty ridiculous and you may laugh at that, but it is not so comical for a person to feel responsible for everything terrible that happens in life. That becomes a totally impossible burden to bear and could lead to self-destructive behavior.

6. Glorification/Martyrdom — Loss can also lead you to say: "All of my struggles and pain show that I am living the way I am supposed to be (the way God wants me to live, according to God's will)." "This is just my row to hoe and I'll do it the best I can." "This is just my cross to bear (deep sigh)." Notice the use of extreme or absolute statements such as the word "all." If you choose to employ this system, you may develop a real martyr complex and take pride in just how much pain and suffering you can endure. Often, you may find yourself throwing "pity parties" to gain sympathy from others. If you find yourself in this type of existence, you may feel sad because there is no joy or possibility in life — just pain and pity.

7. Evil/Warfare — Be careful if you hear yourself saying: "Everything that happens to me is a result of some unseen warfare over which I have no control." Again, take note of the absolute, "everything." This is another extremist stance which allows you to blame someone or something else for all the problems you encounter. The ultimate result of using this system is that you do not have to take responsibility for your own choices or life. Obviously, there are things which happen over which you have no control, but everything? You do have control over your responses to the things that happen to you. This system seeks to eliminate all personal responsibility in life and make human beings puppets in a play. The end result can be living constantly in the "victim" role.

Again, you may, from time to time, find yourself using statements similar to the ones I have listed for you. It is only natural for you to feel any of these ways occasionally and to use statements similar to the ones detailed. However, as stated earlier, the dangers grow when the systems become your primary way of approaching the process of mourning.

I encourage you to be aware of these warning signs as you look for more positive, pro-active approaches to handling your grief.

Now let's move on to Good Mourning!

EARLY MOURNING — THE LOSS EVENT

"The Loss Event," the death of your loved one, has caused your life to change drastically!   Whether you have had time to prepare for the death (a long-term illness) or whether the death came about suddenly and unexpectedly (accident, violence, heart attack, etc.), things as you knew them will never be the same again. I know that this reality is not a pleasant one to face, but it is one which cannot be escaped. Life has definitely changed! Right now you may be faced with an almost overwhelming sense of loss and misdirection. This is to be expected at a time like this.

As a result of "The Loss Event," you will find yourself in the beginnings of the mourning process, which may be referred to as The Early Mourning Phase. During this time, you will receive encouragement and support from friends and family while you begin facing your grief and making many important decisions required following the death of your loved one.

Let's look first at some of the characteristics of Early Mourning.

THE CHARACTERISTICS OF EARLY MOURNING

*T*he process of grieving the loss of a loved one is very difficult. A variety of emotions can and will be experienced as you mourn this loss. The emotions described in this phase of mourning are meant to be representative and are the primary ones felt in the Early Mourning Phase. Just because an emotion is mentioned here does not mean that it cannot be experienced in another phase — on the contrary, overlapping can and does occur in each phase. As you read on, you may be able to grasp what you can expect from yourself and other grieving individuals — whether friends or family members — as you begin the work of mourning your loss.

Shock and a Feeling of Numbness

Initially, a strong sense of shock and a feeling of numbness may occur. These feelings are common and may provide you with a sort of "cushion" from the pain and reality of the loss. This shock and numbness can allow your mind to catch up with the brutal reality of the loss and prepare you to move through the funeral and the first few weeks of the Early Mourning Phase of your grief.

Mechanical Responses

Closely related to the initial shock and numbness, which are likely to occur, is the phenomenon of responding to daily tasks and demands in mechanical ways. It is almost as if you are a wind-up toy as you move through a daily routine which is different from your usual one. In the early stages, this can also be a blessing in disguise. In the hours and days following the death of your loved one and prior to the actual funeral, your responses to the many people who surround you may be perceived as rather robot-like. So often, people who do not understand this part of the grieving process will comment on your strength and how well you are doing. They may not be aware of what is actually going on inside you. Sometimes in the early going, there may be a lack of readily observable emotion, which may give others the false impression that everything is going along fine. The truth is that your body, mind and emotions are protecting and insulating you from the horrible pain, allowing you to move steadily into the reality of your loss.

Disbelief and Denial

A sense of disbelief and denial of the reality of your situation are also natural parts of the early phase of the grieving process. It is so difficult to come to grips with the fact that one whom you loved so much is no longer with you physically. This disbelief and denial are signs that you are beginning to try to deal with the harsh reality facing you. You want things to be different — you want them to go back to the way they were. You may feel that you are in a dream and that you will wake up soon and all will be back to "normal." Unfortunately, you are not in a dream and the reality of the loss must be faced.

Confusion and Disorientation

Yet another characteristic of the Early Mourning Phase is a sense of confusion and disorientation. These feelings are common components of this phase of grieving, and each individual can experience confusion and disorientation in different ways based on a number of variables. Questions as to why this tragedy had to happen to you and your family, how you will be able to go on without your loved one, and how you will face the many changes ahead are common ones asked during this time. Please give yourself permission to ask such questions — they can open the door for you to begin to deal with your loss in healthy ways. Don't expect yourself to "have everything together" — it is perfectly normal to feel confused and disoriented — to not have all the answers.

Isolation and Withdrawal

You may also experience the desire and need to isolate yourself and withdraw from decisions, people, responsibilities and pressures for a while. This, too, is a common response to the initial distress of dealing with the loss of a loved one. The ability to withdraw for reflection and introspection can be helpful as you seek to determine which way you will go from this point forward. Understand, and help others who care about you to understand, that this desire to pull away is common and not to be feared. This isolation can be a source of strength for you — seek to use the "alone time" you experience to begin getting in touch with your thoughts and feelings.

Anger and Betrayal

During this early phase of your mourning, you may also experience feelings of anger and betrayal. Your anger may be closely connected to the "why" questions mentioned earlier. You may be angry at God, yourself, a doctor, the situation, another relative or person connected with the loss of your loved one. You may also feel you have been betrayed by life. This sense of betrayal can be connected to the lost and shattered dreams, goals, hopes and plans you may have shared with your loved one. You may even feel betrayed by or angry with your loved one for leaving you behind. These feelings of anger and betrayal are perfectly normal and are to be expected. Try to find healthy and helpful ways to express your feelings, but try not to get down on yourself if you occasionally express them in unhealthy ways. People around you will probably understand and be supportive of your need to express your emotions at this time. We'll look more at anger in Section Two, The Characteristics of Mid-Mourning.

THE CHALLENGES OF EARLY MOURNING

*G*enerally, the Early Mourning Phase lasts from the time you learn about the death of your loved one through the final disposition of the body; for some, this period can extend as long as three to six weeks after the funeral. During this time period, you will be faced with three unique challenges.

Getting Through the Funeral

The first challenge is that of getting through the funeral. Within a few hours after the notification of the death of your loved one, funeral arrangements must be made. This can be an extremely stressful time for you and your family. Contact with a funeral director will take place at the funeral home itself or in your own home. Decisions must be made regarding the type of service desired and who will officiate, as well as the location of the service, visitation or calling hours, and the method of final disposition of the body. Next comes the contacting of family members, friends and co-workers.

Usually, there is a span of a few days from the time of death to the actual funeral. Often during this time, concerned, caring and loving individuals will contact you with their condolences and offers of assistance. Allow them to care for and nurture you and your family. This outpouring of help and love is a vital part of the mourning rituals necessary for the beginnings of good, healthy mourning.

The day of the funeral can be a very difficult one for everyone involved. It is a time to say goodbye to your loved one. The feelings of pain, loneliness, despair and loss are almost indescribable. Anticipate that you may be overwhelmed by these emotions. Do not feel badly about your need to express those feelings through tears, hugs and words. Give yourself permission to express your sense of loss in any way with which you feel comfortable.

"Getting through" the funeral is probably the best way to describe the first challenge in the Early Mourning Phase. You will literally "get through" it in the best way you possibly can. No matter how much care and planning goes into the actual funeral service, it can be extremely difficult. You are saying goodbye to a loved one for the last time.

At this time, care and support from friends and family members can be of utmost importance. Do not be afraid to lean heavily on them for emotional, mental, spiritual and physical support. Ask for what you need from those around you who are willing and able to give. It is during this time that people are most willing to assist you — they want to help you. Let them! In so doing, you will be able to more successfully meet the first challenge of the Early Mourning Phase — getting through the funeral.

Dealing With First Things

Following the funeral, you will be faced with the second challenge of the Early Mourning Phase — that of dealing with the "first things" necessary in putting all your loved one's papers and affairs in order. These tasks will demand your attention. You may find that you will need the assistance of a caring, understanding and knowledgeable friend or family member to help organize all the paperwork ahead of you. Again, this is a perfect time to ask for and receive help. The shock and numbness will still be present to a certain degree as you begin making the calls and writing the letters required to settle estate matters, insurance matters, Social Security claims, etc. (For more guidance on these arrangements, please turn to Appendix A, page 89.)

During this period of activity, your focus will be on "taking care of details" which may not give you as much time to work on the issues of your personal grief as you would like. Try to re-frame this activity period and look at it as one of the steps you must take in the process of mourning your loss. Handling these details may provide you with a sense of closure, and at times, a unique sense of closeness to your loved one.

This time may also give you the opportunity to reflect on the relationship you had with your loved one which now only exists in memory. Many of these memories will be positive and uplifting. While taking care of details, you may find yourself both crying and laughing as you share your thoughts and memories with friends and family members. This sharing can form the foundation of your continued grief work as you move through the mourning process.

Not all relationships are perfect, and you may discover some mental and emotional dissonance as you reflect. Do not be afraid of seemingly contradictory emotions and thoughts — these are common for persons facing a deep loss. Make note of these feelings, thoughts and experiences and then plan to talk with someone about them as soon as possible. Realize that as you face this challenge, you will not only put closure on some aspects of your grief, you will also be opening the door to the next steps in your journey through Good Mourning.

Preparing for the Transitions to Come

The third challenge facing you in the Early Mourning Phase is that of preparing for the transitions to come.

Following the harried activity surrounding the funeral and the almost constant attention you will receive from people who care for you, you will naturally move into a period of adjustment without your loved one. As much as you want the whole world to recognize that your life has been forever changed and to give you time to stop and make adjustments, the simple fact of the matter is that life goes on.

Those who hovered so close to you in the early days after the loss and possibly those who helped you handle the details of settling the affairs of your loved one will get back to their routine — that is to be expected. Now comes the beginning of the period of transitions and intense grief work. Although you can receive help from friends, family members, support groups and professional counselors and therapists, the grief work facing you will be your own.

This third challenge is possibly the most important of the Early Mourning Phase in that as you face it, you will be preparing yourself to begin making necessary choices in the mourning process. Know that transitions await you. As you approach them, realize, too, that you have choices and options as to how you negotiate these changes. This realization can provide you with a certain sense of freedom as you move through the process of mourning your loss.

THE CHOICES OF
EARLY MOURNING

*D*eath causes us to face the fact of our mortality in a way no other experience does. When you are touched by the death of a loved one, the myth of being in control of things is brutally shattered. You may suddenly feel very vulnerable, weak and victimized. This sense of being out of control can be so overwhelming at times that it can potentially paralyze your thoughts, feelings and actions.

Although you cannot control what life gives you, you can choose your responses.

In making CHOICES, you can begin to regain a sense of control over life in a different way than you had before the death. This sense of control can help you focus on how you respond to life's events. It can help you look at yourself and your life in a more realistic manner.

You do not have to simply be a helpless victim in the path of an unmerciful world, steamrolled by its hit-and-run tactics. You can become more pro-active as you handle things and therefore begin to act more responsibly toward yourself and life. You can begin to make a difference for yourself and others through the gift of choice. The Early Mourning Phase carries with it three unique choices which must be pondered.

The Choice of Acknowledgement, Acceptance And Affirmation

The first choice is one which begins almost at an unconscious level after you learn of your loved one's death. This choice has three components — Acknowledgement, Acceptance and Affirmation. The first two components are to Acknowledge the death of your loved one and begin to move toward Accepting that reality. Although shock and numbness surround you initially, at some level you are beginning to process the reality of the death. One of the first steps in acknowledging and accepting this reality involves talking about what has happened and working at completing the necessary practical tasks mentioned earlier (*see page 24*). These activities may ease you into the aspects of acknowledgement and acceptance of the death.

The third component which may help you make this first choice easier is that of Affirmation. As you begin to acknowledge and accept the reality of the death, you can help yourself by affirming those things which remain. Begin by affirming that you are here and that you have unique individual strengths and abilities upon which to draw as you face this difficult situation. Also, affirm the positive accomplishments in which you may have participated with your loved one — children, business development, contributions to society, educational accomplishments, etc. These joint accomplishments can give you a sense of connection with and pride in the relationship.

Another area for possible affirmation lies in plans jointly made for the future — i.e., life insurance plans, annuity programs, educational provisions, etc. These may help you affirm your ability to move ahead in life despite this devastating blow. Plans made with the future in mind can provide a true sense of connection with and continuity of the relationship. Affirm your friends, your family members, your life!

The Choice to Mourn the Loss Fully

The second option you face is the choice to mourn the loss fully. It is imperative that this choice be examined in the Early Mourning Phase because of the way in which our society discourages grieving the loss of a loved one.

Generally, society feels that death is something to be denied — it can and must be overcome somehow. For this reason, society will not readily encourage or allow you to mourn your loss in healthy and constructive ways. Obviously, each individual situation is different, and you may have a wonderful support system which allows and encourages healthy mourning, but society as a whole does a poor job of permitting you to grieve and assisting you in this process. This being the case, you must choose to mourn your loss in the most healthy ways you can.

Grief is an emotion, and thus needs to be expressed and not stored or repressed inside. Give yourself permission to feel the emotions connected with grieving and to express them and heal your hurt. Repressed or unexpressed grief can have serious detrimental effects on your emotional, mental, physical and spiritual well-being. As your grief is expressed, it will gradually be drained.

You can choose to express your grief in many healthy ways, including tears, laughter, quiet contemplation, art, work, play, exercise, talk, touch, writing, reading and prayer, just to name a few. Once you choose to mourn your loss, you will employ a combination of activities which are unique for you.

As you express your sadness and grief in your own way, seek to resist being overly directed by other — usually well-meaning — people as to how you should or should not express your grief. Mourning is an individual process—find ways which work for you as you express your grief.

The Choice to Embrace the Pain of Mourning

The third choice you face in this Early Mourning Phase is that of embracing the pain of mourning. Once you have chosen to begin the acknowledgement/acceptance/affirmation cycle of this phase and have chosen to fully mourn your loss through healthy expression of your feelings, you are then ready to face this third choice. At some level, you are aware that there can be tremendous pain associated with mourning the loss of a loved one.

I choose the analogy of embracing on purpose. I have never liked "partial embraces" — give me a good, full, bear-hug embrace any time. Partial embraces communicate hesitancy, fear, mistrust, disinterest and any number of other messages which cause you to be tentative in approaching a person. Yet, a full embrace — even when there has been a misunderstanding or a difference of opinion between people — communicates full acceptance and a willingness to "work things through." When you choose to embrace the pain of mourning, you are choosing to accept the responsibilities and consequences of your actions as you mourn this loss. A full embrace leaves no lingering questions about what exists in any relationship. The same is true when you embrace the pain of mourning.

Dealing with pain — whether emotional, mental, physical or spiritual — can be terribly frightening. This choice sets the stage for you to move into the next phase of your mourning journey — a phase where your most intense grief work will be undertaken. Realize that when you choose to embrace the pain of mourning, you will suffer the pain of the many emotions which accompany the loss of a loved one.

Additionally, this choice includes enduring the suffering over a period of time. Good mourning does not happen overnight — it takes time.

The passing of time, however — in and of itself — does not cause you to heal. The key to healing lies in what you choose to do with the time you have. Both the process of mourning and time are commodities which must be invested to affect your life in healthy ways. When you choose to suffer and endure the pain of mourning over the long haul, you have chosen the path to healthy resolution of your grief.

Efforts to avoid the pain of mourning can only bring with them the potential for even greater pain in the future. I encourage you to be realistic about this embrace. You are embracing the pain of mourning and you will suffer — yet as you endure this suffering, the healthy resolution of your grief can be helped along in ways which can produce positive results for you and your family.

MOVING INTO MID-MOURNING — THE TRANSITION

*O*nce you have negotiated the difficult first days of the funeral and have handled the details discussed in Appendix A of this book, you will enter into the Mid-Mourning or Transition Phase of the mourning process. This phase may be characterized by the intense grief work which comes into play. The importance of this phase cannot be emphasized enough — for the way in which you go through this phase can have a tremendous effect on how you are able to continue on with your life.

If you choose to push back the feelings associated with or ignore the issues relating to the Mid-Mourning transition period, it is likely that your continuation of life will be colored by these choices in negative ways.

If, on the other hand, you choose to engage in healthy grief work in this transition phase, you may be able to move along with your life in much more healthy and positive ways. Obviously, the choice is yours.

This section will provide a framework in which to examine your options as you continue to deal with your loss.

THE CHARACTERISTICS OF MID-MOURNING

*A*s the cards, letters and calls become less frequent and as the lives of those who were there for you in the early stages of your ordeal begin to get back to normal, yours will not. You will find yourself faced with the harsh reality of the loss you have suffered.

Often, people will mistakenly believe that the most difficult time in a loss situation comes in the early stages and will respond in kind. This is not the truth. Often, the time you need support the most will be the time it is least available.

You may find yourself facing much of this time alone as you seek to find some semblance of order and normalcy. It is important to understand some of the major characteristic emotions and situations you will face in this transition. Again, the emotions and situations mentioned here may be experienced in any of the phases, but typically characterize this middle phase.

Deep Separation Pain or Anxiety

As the reality of the loss begins to sink in, you may experience a deep separation pain or anxiety. You realize that the person you lost will never return to you physically. A deep sense of yearning for the person may set in and you may also experience a longing to be with that person, or a longing for things to be as they were before the loss. Sometimes this yearning and longing can become so intense that you may try to bargain with God, the stars, or other powers in which you believe, to make things the way they were. This wishing or bargaining is also prevalent in anticipatory grief, such as with a loved one experiencing an extended illness. It is important to understand, however, that while these feelings are a perfectly normal part of grieving, this is still a form of magical thinking which cannot alter reality in any way.

Difficulty Distinguishing Fact from Fantasy

Along with the separation pain and anxiety can come a need to identify with the loved one to the point that you may experience difficulty in distinguishing fact from fantasy. Often, dreams involving the deceased, hallucinations of seeing the deceased in a familiar setting, and imagining that you hear the person walking or speaking can occur. These experiences can seem very real and, at times, can be rather unsettling. Please know that these experiences are common to many and are not a sign that you are losing touch with reality. It is no surprise that you may become confused at times as you try to sort through the emotions you are facing. Everything may seem to be in a state of disarray. I encourage you to allow yourself to experience these situations and try not to ignore or repress them. In doing so, you will enable yourself to move along in a healthy manner.

Physical Symptoms

It is likely that you may experience physical symptoms connected with your grieving. Sleep disturbances, reduced appetite, anxiety attacks, headaches, stomach aches and shortness of breath are common physical symptoms experienced by persons in this phase of the mourning process. You may also be more susceptible to illness since you are likely to be physically exhausted at times and your immune system weakened. It is advisable for you to contact your family physician as soon as possible for assistance in monitoring your health.

Flooding of Emotions

As the reality of your loss continues to sink in, you are likely to experience a flooding of emotions — many times, more intensely than you have ever experienced before. Occasionally, it may be difficult to distinguish one emotion from another due to the fact that they may all be battling for attention and expression. It may feel like the dam has broken and you are in danger of drowning in the flood. Try to allow yourself to feel and express those emotions as they come — knowing that seeking to repress them can be unhealthy.

Intense Sadness and Loneliness

Feelings of intense sadness and loneliness are likely to occur as the reality of the loss drives itself into your consciousness. These emotions can be overwhelming at times and can cause you to feel completely helpless and lost.

You may find yourself struggling with the decision to be around people or seek solitude when you feel lonely and sad. Even in the presence of others, you may still experience a sense of loneliness. For this reason, you may often find yourself choosing to avoid gatherings of any size — "What good is it if I still feel lonely when I am with others?" is a question often asked by people in your situation.

At times, you may feel like you have to mask your sadness when you are around others and pretend that everything is fine. I encourage you, instead, to risk being with people and allow yourself to express this sadness in their presence. Both you and those around you may benefit from these expressions of feeling. You may find release and they may learn to be more at ease around you.

Seeking to be with people when you are feeling sad and lonely can be a gift to them and to you. Everyone going through this phase needs gifts to help ease the pain.

Guilt Feelings

Guilt is another common emotion characteristic of the Mid-Mourning Phase of grief. You may find yourself feeling guilty about being the one left behind or about not doing enough to show your love for the deceased before he or she died. You may also feel guilty about having received an inheritance or insurance settlement following the death. You may feel guilty about not being able to fully follow through on promises you may have made to your loved one before he or she died.

Guilt can also come from the mistaken belief that the death of your loved one is some sort of punishment to you for something you either did or did not do; it may also come because of fleeting thoughts or wishes that your loved one would die — magical thinking again; guilt may be connected to your perception that you have done something "terrible," "stupid," or "inappropriate" following the death of your loved one.

You may be able to convince yourself to feel guilty about almost anything connected with the death of your loved one, regardless of how illogical the thought or situation may be. Guilt can be either real or false. Often, the guilt felt by survivors is false guilt and is a learned behavior or habit. You would be wise to talk with someone who understands this "guilt phenomenon" and challenge those illogical guilt thoughts and feelings. Realize that if you feel guilty in any way connected with the death of your loved one, you need to take steps to talk these thoughts and feelings through with someone who cares and understands.

Guilt feelings are common in the aftermath of a death — but not all guilt is justified. Try to find ways to determine which kind of guilt you are experiencing and then deal with it appropriately.

Feelings of Depression

Often, you may feel depressed as the reality becomes more apparent in your daily life. Depression is another common response to your loss. Many days, you may feel like staying in bed and not going anywhere or doing anything with anyone. When you feel depressed, you may not have energy for much of anything else. Mourning takes a tremendous amount of energy.

Depression is to be expected as you work through your mourning process. You may feel weak, disinterested, have a "heavy feeling" in your chest, you may cry often and unexpectedly, you may feel totally empty. Your thoughts may center on the uselessness of life and living and your perceived unworthiness as a person. All these experiences are a part of normal depression following the loss of a loved one, and although it may not appear so now, this depression will pass. You are not having a breakdown and your feelings are not a sign of weakness. This depression is part of what you need to say your goodbye to your loved one.

One word of caution: if you feel yourself becoming chronically depressed and you cannot seem to pull yourself out of your depression through grief activities such as talking, exercise, writing, etc., you may need to visit with a professional who can help. Remember that you must take care of yourself to successfully go through the mourning process.

Feelings of Powerlessness, Abandonment and Victimization Resulting in Anger and Rage

Anger and rage are also common responses to loss. As the reality of the loss becomes more apparent in your life, the anger and rage you may feel can deepen and intensify.

Your anger can be aimed at any number of "targets." You may feel anger toward the person who died; you may feel anger toward God for either "taking your loved one away from you" or for not doing anything to keep him or her alive; your anger may be directed toward a doctor or medical staff; you may find yourself angry at people not connected to the death in any way; you may discover that you are angry with yourself for something you perceive that you could or should have done before your loved one died.

Your anger may turn into a type of rage as you seek to find someone or something to "blame" for the death. You might find yourself wanting to strike out verbally or physically. Many times, in an effort to deal with the intense feelings of anger and rage, you may displace your anger by expressing it toward someone or something not related to your loss.

To a great degree, this anger stems from feeling powerless, abandoned and victimized. God, the world, all the forces of the universe have teamed up against you and have taken a precious possession. What can you do?

Many times, people think that simply feeling anger and rage and expressing those feelings in random and unfocused ways are their only outlets. Often, these random expressions only compound the feelings of powerlessness and victimization.

It is perfectly acceptable to express your feelings verbally and physically — to vent them — as long as you do not present a potential harm to yourself, others or property. In addition to expressing your feelings through writing, physical activity, therapy or group support, you may find some relief by taking constructive action to improve the situation connected with the death of your loved one or to raise community awareness in some positive way. Examples might include: establishing a support group for individuals in situations similar to yours, requesting that educational resources be made available to individuals in a similar situation, establishing a scholarship fund in memory of your loved one, etc.

Remember, however, that there are also dangers in over-involving yourself in causes — activity is good as long as you don't make it a substitute for, or allow it to mask, your real feelings. To work through your grief in a complete way, it is important that you face your feelings while engaging in constructive expressions of emotion.

The key point is that feelings of anger and rage are to be expected. You are encouraged to express that anger and rage in appropriate, helpful ways. As you express those emotions, they will be drained and you will be on the road to recovery. In constructively expressing anger, you will also begin regaining a sense of power and control and become better able to fight the feelings of helplessness and victimization.

Feelings of Fear and Panic

A final pair of emotions characteristic of the Mid-Mourning Phase of grief are fear and panic. At times, you may be faced with an overwhelming sense of fear that something dreadful is about to happen to you or someone you love. This sense of fear and panic can produce some very real physical, mental and emotional symptoms. Realize that you have real reasons for feeling this way. You have just faced the most devastating of all human experiences, the death of a loved one.

You may feel extremely vulnerable and weak. You may feel the need to "lock yourself away" from the world and its dangers. Again, these are normal feelings during this phase of intense grief.

Try not to be afraid or avoid these feelings of fear and panic. Instead, seek ways to allow yourself to express your feelings constructively. This may allow you to begin facing your fears — both known and unknown — so that you can continue moving on in your process of mourning.

THE CHALLENGES OF
MID-MOURNING

*T*he Mid-Mourning Phase may best be described as a period of working out your grief. The picture which comes to mind is one of a weight room, equipped with weights, stationary bicycles, stair-step machines, treadmills, mirrors, scales, jump ropes, etc. I see a picture of a person entering the room and determining which equipment will be used for that particular day's workout. The person realizes that this workout will require effort and that a certain amount of time will be involved. The person also realizes that in order for the workouts to be of any use or produce the intended outcome, they must be done on a consistent basis. The idea of getting into shape through working out brings with it the concepts of involvement, effort, patience, time, fatigue, frustration and, finally, accomplishment. The physical, emotional, mental and spiritual benefits of exercise are widely known.

In like manner, going through a time of working out your grief can bring about the same benefits as physical exercise.

This Mid-Mourning or Transition Phase of grief also includes effort, involvement, patience, time, fatigue, frustration and accomplishment. Can you imagine going into a gym, being dressed to work out, and then just sitting and looking at the machines, asking them to get you in shape without putting forth any effort? Neither can I! That would seem rather ridiculous, wouldn't it? Yet, many people enter this part of the process with that kind of attitude. This is the most difficult part of the entire process — the part which demands the most from you.

It would be great if you could just skip this part and move on to the final phase. The only problem is that for you to continue on with your life in a healthy, integrated manner, you must go through the "workout" part of the process. Otherwise, you could carry unresolved issues of grief with you, adversely affecting all areas of your relationships and responsibilities in the future.

In keeping with this workout theme, you will face four specific challenges in the Mid-Mourning Phase of your grief. And, just as the bodybuilder works out different muscle groups in the gym, you will tackle each of these challenges individually as part of your total body workout. These workout challenges can be defined as Undoing, Checking Your Reality, Finding Stability and Structuring Your Grief.

How long will these visits to the gym last before you are ready to move on to the next phase? I'm not really sure. Some have indicated that it takes from two to four years to fully grieve the death of a loved one. This intense period of grief is neither completely predictable nor determined by specific time-frames. Many factors and variables can impact your progress. Yet, with healthy grief work, you may begin experiencing a noticeable difference and healing between six months to one year following the death.

With healthy mourning, you may begin to see and feel the changes necessary to moving on with your life. In other words, during this time of intense grief workouts, you will be making the transitions necessary to continue on in a healthy manner — emotionally, mentally, physically and spiritually.

Let's now examine each challenge, or workout area, separately.

Undoing

The first challenge of this phase is in the area of Undoing, or disconnecting from the relationship which now exists only in memory. This does not mean disconnecting from the emotions surrounding the loss — those must be dealt with and expressed. What this does mean is working on the reality that your loved one has indeed died and that you will not have the privilege of seeing and being with that person physically ever again. It means that you must begin to divest emotional energy from that relationship in order to begin focusing that energy on yourself, your family and your future.

This is a very difficult challenge to face simply because you have a history — a pattern of relating to your loved one which has been established over time. Often, you may find yourself trying to figure out ways to make things the way they used to be — or at least wishing you could make them change. You may find yourself expending great amounts of time and energy in this fantasy exercise. Recall some of the characteristics mentioned earlier in this section. Do you see how important it is to begin the process of Undoing without repressing the emotions which go along with grieving? Undoing means that you must start looking realistically at who you are, what resources you have, which directions you now want to follow, and how you can best integrate what remains of the lost relationship into your life.

Checking Your Reality

The second challenge which must be encountered is that of checking your reality. This challenge involves the monitoring of your personal efforts to distinguish between the loss event which has occurred and your responses to that loss. In a sense, it is an extension of the first challenge mentioned — that of undoing. As you work to divest emotional energy from the relationship which has been lost and try to find ways to invest that energy elsewhere, you will need a way to check the nature of the reality in which you are now living. These checks are likely to occur through two distinct, yet related, activities — reviewing and sorting through the relationship.

Living in the reality of the "here and now" demands that we review the relationship we had with our loved one. The relationship has changed — it is now a relationship in memory rather than activity. It is no longer growing and developing. It is a captive of thought, pictures, words, perceptions and experiences — all of which are accessible for review and reflection. Realize that in addition to the positive aspects of the relationship, the review process may uncover areas which can also be painful. People are not perfect and, therefore, relationships are not perfect. You are likely to go back to the very beginning of your relationship and review each aspect — each event — to evaluate them according to the significance and value each holds for you. The reality of things said and not said, things completed and things left unfinished — unfulfilled dreams, hopes and plans — will all be reviewed.

You may also discover that there were things about the person and relationship of which you were not particularly fond. These unpleasant memories also surface in the review process. The importance of conducting the relationship review lies in being able to sharpen the clarity of the relationship — what it meant and still means to you; what things were useful and what things were hindering; which areas were fulfilling and which areas were stifling; which areas produced regret, guilt and suffering, as well as pride, comfort and strength.

It is not uncommon for a survivor to place the lost loved one and relationship they shared on a "pedestal of perfection" — one which cannot be compared or replaced. Since perfection does not exist, it is imperative that you look honestly at both the person and the relationship to gain a clear picture of the reality in which you now find yourself. Once you have constructed a clear, realistic picture of the relationship, you may find yourself better able to differentiate the useful from the useless, the exciting from the mundane, the enriching from the discounting, the warm from the cold, and the happy from the sad of the relationship — all of which are parts of every significant relationship.

This picture will help you tackle the second part of checking your reality — sorting through the relationship.

In reviewing, you list the good, bad and indifferent — every aspect of your relationship with your loved one. You look at each aspect in a broad sense but don't assign a weight, or importance, of one over another. In the next step, sorting through the relationship, you take the information retrieved in the review process and "sort through" the various aspects you uncovered. It becomes more specific, a little like separating your clothes on wash day.

To look your best in your clothes, you must separate them before cleaning. You separate the whites from the colors, the perma press from the delicate, the hand-washables from the clothes to be dry cleaned or professionally laundered. Throwing all of your clothes together and treating them the same on wash day can produce disastrous results — the same can be true if you fail to sort through your memories. Not all memories carry the same weight — and not all memories and experiences need the same amount or type of attention. As you "sort through" your memories and experiences, you will begin measuring and assigning importance to each. Analysis and careful examination are important to this process.

At this point, your real grief begins to take shape and form. You will probably want to carry some of the best parts of the relationship and its influences on with you as you continue to live following the loss.

You may also discover that you will be able to uncover mistakes made in this relationship and learn valuable lessons which can be carried with you as you progress through your grief.

Sorting through the relationship can also allow you to determine areas of your lifestyle and relationship patterns which need to be changed, discarded or eliminated to help ensure healthy recovery and continuation.

Through the total process of reviewing and sorting, you will examine pleasant memories, painful memories, aspects of the relationship with your loved one that you will always save and aspects that are best let go. Remember that all experiences impact you both positively and negatively — you must decide for yourself how much each memory or experience will affect your life from this day on.

The challenge of Checking Your Reality requires you to review your relationship, sort through the experiences and select which influences you will carry with you as you continue your journey.

Finding Stability

The third challenge of the Mid-Mourning Phase is that of finding stability. The Mid-Mourning Phase brings with it a tremendous amount of disorganization and confusion. Nothing is the same as it was before the loss event. You may feel differently about yourself, your status, your family, your relationships, your roles — everything has changed.

You may perceive that people treat you differently than before. They may try to smother you with attention and advice, or you may feel abandoned by them. As strange as it may seem, both may be true. Often, people will go to both extremes in an attempt to either deal with their own discomfort about death and mortality brought on by the death of your loved one, or their own ambivalent feelings toward you. In either case, their responses and actions can contribute to your sense of disorganization and confusion. In light of this, the need for a sense of stability may become more acute.

Finding stability refers to the challenge of restructuring all of your relationships — both interpersonal and intra-personal — from the perspective of a person changed by the death of a loved one. This challenge may be compounded by others who are dependent on you in some way — children, grandchildren, siblings, spouse, other family members — who are also experiencing their own grief and will look to you for strength, guidance and support.

Because your most intense grief work will be conducted during this phase, much of your energy will naturally be focused on you. The presence of other dependents requires you to also focus some of that energy on them; however, you must realize that finding stability for yourself will ultimately provide an atmosphere and model of stability for those dependent on you. This realization may help you feel better about directing attention toward yourself so you can then better focus on the needs of those dependents. Remember, it is only in finding stability for yourself that you create the foundation for others who depend on you to find their own ways of healing.

You are different now than you were before the loss of your loved one. You will never be the same — neither will those close to you and your family. The challenge of finding stability means that you must face the differences within yourself, your family and your world realistically. To find stability, you may need to learn new approaches to decision making and problem solving, discover different areas from which to draw support, and explore meaningful new ways to relate to the world around you.

The challenge of finding stability requires you to face yourself in a way you may never have considered before now. This challenge to begin rebuilding a new life is not unlike the challenge faced by those whose property, belongings and work have been destroyed by a natural disaster. Experiencing the death of a loved one is like being a survivor in the devastation of an earthquake, the terror of a hurricane or the fury of a tornado. You are left to start over, and you must begin by finding stability for the grueling task ahead.

Structuring Your Grief

The fourth challenge you will face in the Mid-Mourning Phase of the grief process is that of structuring your grief. Grief is not something that can be wrapped in a neat package, complete with instructions and guarantees — thoroughly predictable and contained. Although the grief process is identifiable, defined and traceable, it is not something which can be passed through quickly and without effort — there are no short cuts or magical formulas to make things easier.

"Structuring" your grief can be very much like the process of making a pot on a potter's wheel. A good friend and therapist introduced me to the concept of "Green Grief" one day as we visited together. He explained that as we mourn the loss of a loved one, we begin to mold or structure our grieving into something with which we are comfortable. In other words, we begin to make sense of our lives as we grieve and mourn the loss.

As we meet the challenges of this particular phase, we open the door to creating a new person out of the process.

A rough pot, vase, bowl or platter has the familiar form of the intended final product, yet it is still very fragile and soft and can be easily cracked, broken or destroyed until it has been fired. In this stage of creation, it is said to be "green ware" — it has yet to reach completion or maturity through the final firing process. Many times, the artist must make adjustments in his or her creation due to impurities in the clay or asymmetry problems before the final firing of the work of art.

Your work of grief and mourning during this phase is very much the same. You are beginning to form a new you as you grieve. You are looking honestly at your relationship with your loved one, yourself, your other relationships, and what it is that you want to do and become. You are structuring a "rough new you."

You will be very fragile and will make some mistakes as you work. You may find yourself making alterations and adjustments to what it is you want to become — you may even have to start over in certain areas. Much like pottery in the "green ware" phase, you are in the "green grief" part of your work— you are learning about yourself in ways you may never have before. You are getting ready for the final firing process.

The Mid-Mourning transition phase provides you with the opportunity to try new and different approaches in discovering who you are and how to best express those discoveries. Be gentle with yourself when you make mistakes. Open the door to experience all the emotions of this particular phase. Give yourself permission to change your mind and grow. Do not be afraid to experience solitude, for it is in solitude that much of your creative work will be done.

The challenge is structuring your grief. The reward is self-knowledge. The outcome is the opportunity to move ahead to the next set of challenges with confidence.

THE CHOICES OF MID-MOURNING

*T*he choices of the Mid-Mourning Phase flow naturally from the challenges just discussed. In this phase, you will have the opportunity to consider three choices as you continue your process of good mourning. You will be able to choose to Be Alone, Assert Yourself and Begin Rebuilding. Each choice requires effort, and the process goes hand-in-hand with the intense grief work associated with this phase. Again, the transition period is crucial to your ability to move ahead with your life in a healthy and useful manner. At first, you may find yourself exploring these choices tentatively — feeling a bit unsure of yourself. This is perfectly natural and you need not feel discouraged if you find yourself struggling with them at times. As with any new activity or skill, the more you practice, the better you become.

The Choice to Be Alone

The choice to Be Alone is one of the most difficult you will ever have to make in this process of mourning. There is something quite fearful in realizing that grief work is very personal and that you are responsible for your own progress. Yet, in order to face the challenges of Mid-Mourning mentioned earlier, you must choose to be alone. This is a choice of true courage — a choice which indicates that you are ready to face the real task of getting on with your life.

You will find yourself alone with your thoughts, feelings and responses. It is a choice to stop the overpursuit of activities which may have previously kept you from looking honestly at your situation. Becoming involved in "busyness" is a common response to loss situations. At first glance, many of these activities carry with them varying degrees of merit. Activities related to work, church involvement, diverse social functions, and activities which call upon you to take care of other — usually weaker — individuals, are all noble endeavors. Yet, the overpursuit of these activities may become a barrier to healthy grief work. Over-participation in these activities may be attempts to forget or push aside what has happened to you.

Additionally, there are dangers in becoming overly-involved in activities which promise the medication or dulling of the pain you are experiencing. Be aware that you may be tempted to try to medicate feelings of pain, loneliness and despair through the use of drugs, alcohol, uncontrolled sexual behaviors, illogical religious rituals, frenetic activity or excessive partying. Pain, in and of itself, is not bad or harmful. Pain can be an indication of an area which needs attention from you. It is extremely difficult to deal with something which needs your attention if you have dulled your senses to that pain.

The choice to Be Alone is a choice to deal realistically with your loss and the pain which accompanies it. It is a time to examine the meanings this loss has in your life — a time to evaluate whether you are reacting or responding to this loss. It is a time to begin taking stock of what you have and are and how you intend to use those discoveries in your future actions and plans.

This is the choice to begin your "wisdom search" as you mourn. By choosing to Be Alone, you gain important insights into yourself, the world around you and your relationships with others. You truly have the opportunity to gain wisdom — wisdom so very necessary as you rebuild your life following your loss.

You must realize that the choice to Be Alone requires that you occasionally isolate yourself from friends and family. You will need time alone to conduct your relationship review and sort through your experiences with your loved one — to discover how you think this whole process has affected you.

The solitude of being alone, however, is more than just a spatial experience — it also encompasses an attitude. Often, you may find yourself among people yet still choosing to be introspective — to think about aspects of your relationship which might surface when triggered by a particular conversation or activity. This, too, is the choice to Be Alone — alone with your thoughts and feelings, even in the presence of others — which is a perfectly natural response.

This choice of being alone and isolating yourself from others can cause some trepidation as well. What if those around you forget that you exist or need company? What if they stop including you in their activities because you appear to be doing "just fine?" What will you do when you need to talk with someone about your thoughts or discoveries and no one is close by?

Obviously, the choice to be alone does not mean that you totally shut yourself away from friends and family. On the contrary, you should seek a sort of balance between your "alone time" and your time with people. You will need people who can serve as sounding boards for some of your thoughts and discoveries. The process of being alone can cause you to be more open to suggestions, books, support group participation, therapy or other relaxing and helpful activities which other survivors have found beneficial in similar circumstances.

The beauty of the choice to be alone lies in the personal discoveries, explorations, questions and alternatives which will evolve as you progress. Books, movies, lectures, plays, discussions with friends can all become springboards for evaluation, re-evaluation, change and discovery.

Again, the choice to be alone is a choice of courage — the courage to look honestly at yourself, the relationship with your loved one, your responses to the loss and where you think you might want to go from here. It is the choice to courageously balance "alone time" and "people time" — both of which are necessary when you choose to Be Alone.

The Choice to Assert Yourself

The second choice of the Mid-Mourning Phase is the choice to Assert Yourself. Asserting yourself means taking a stand, making a positive statement or making a declaration. This, too, is a choice of courage because these assertions can often be made in the face of some degree of opposition — either from yourself or others around you.

As stated previously, you are a different person following your loss. Just how different you are and will become are directly related to the discoveries you make about yourself in your "alone times." In choosing to Assert Yourself, you must take all the information revealed in those times of reflection and decide who you are, what you want to become and how you plan to get there. These decisions will be made known in the form of life assertions. In making these life assertions, you will decide to take responsibility for yourself, your actions and your future. This entire process may be encapsulated in the word "change."

The process of asserting yourself begins with a change in your thinking, which ultimately emerges in positive actions. In the very beginning of the mourning process, you may feel unable to go on with your life following the devastating event. Feelings of despair, loneliness and longing tend to reinforce these thoughts. During the process of evaluation, however, you uncover a tremendous amount of information about yourself, your relationship and your world. This is all done on a day-by-day basis.

After a period of discovery, you may realize that you have been living and growing and making decisions — maybe doing things for and by yourself that you never dreamed possible. You may also realize that you have begun to think differently about yourself and the world in which you live.

At this point in the process, you may begin thinking, "I just may live through this loss — no, I WILL live through this loss." At this point, you will have proof that you do have the ability and resources to move ahead and live life, albeit a different life, than before. You may also think, "I will incorporate this loss into the fabric of my life and rebuild a new one."

These changes in thought are essential to Asserting Yourself as a person capable of good mourning. Once you begin to change your thought processes, your feelings about your future and your possibilities will follow.

You may experience any number of emotions as you encounter the prospects of moving on — at first, anxiety, fear, sadness, longing, and then excitement, anticipation, feelings of success and accomplishment, as you become increasingly comfortable with the new you. Once your thoughts and feelings confirm your ability to move on, they will be expressed in positive actions.

A word of caution here is that there are a few hurdles which must be overcome in this choice. These hurdles are temptation, fear and selection.

The first hurdle you must face is the temptation to remain a victim of the loss. Feelings of victimization are common to those facing the death of a loved one. Nothing brings feelings of victimization to the surface easier than death. You may ask such questions as, "Why us? Why now? What did I do to deserve this?" You feel out of control, picked on and used in a cruel sort of way.

Generally, there are individuals around who can and will lend support as you try to make sense of this senseless intrusion into your life. Often, these folks will be around for long periods of time and find real personal comfort in "taking care" of you in your distress. Admittedly, it feels good to have people around who can and will take care of you and your family.

As good as this feels, however, it is not in your best interest to be completely taken care of for the rest of your life. Remaining a victim of the loss means that you must constantly keep your supply of "care-takers" full. It means that you must always find people who are willing to feel sorry for you — to pity your plight — and step in and "do for you." It means that you will spend most of your energy building a wall of human beings who will help you keep the reality from getting through and keep you from taking responsibility for your own life.

Although there is a certain amount of comfort in the victim role for a time, the truth is that this role can be debilitating. When you cross the hurdle of remaining the victim — or helpless mourner — you run the risk of having to face the situation completely and become responsible for yourself. This can be both frightening and disconcerting. That is why the temptation to remain the victim of the loss is so great.

You may not always know what to do or how to respond in every situation — indeed, you may make some mistakes. On the surface, it would seem easier to have someone else take responsibility for your life. You would always have someone else to blame if or when things did not go exactly right. Yet, once you cross this hurdle of temptation and decide not to remain the victim, you will be ready to risk taking responsibility for yourself — a risk essential to your survival and progress.

The fear of how others might respond to you asserting yourself as a new, different and responsible person is the second hurdle which must be crossed. You may find yourself worrying about how friends, family members, social acquaintances, work associates or society in general will respond to the you which is emerging as a result of this mourning process. Your perceptions of how others see your progress can be very powerful in keeping you from moving on.

Realize that people will have "advice" about everything you are facing and deciding. Most people who give advice expect you to follow it without question and may become angry if you do not. It is easy for others to criticize your decisions and actions from the outside — they are not living your experience. You may find that this pressure from worrying about how others might respond to your changes will keep you from trying things you want to try. Not only are you faced with your fear about how they will respond, you are also fearful of not doing the "right thing."

It is important for you to realize that the death of your loved one has not just impacted your life — it has impacted others around you as well. Often, people will seek to exert pressure on you to keep you where you are for their own purposes. They may feel uncomfortable with the changes they perceive taking place in you. They may even feel pressure to change their own responses to life because of your changes. However, you must not allow the fear of how others might respond to your changes to deter you from moving on with your life. Your life is yours to live! You have the sole responsibility for how it will be lived! Only you can truly decide how to handle your life! Crossing this hurdle is difficult, but once it is done, it can open the door to continued healthy grieving and a healthy perspective on your abilities to care for yourself and your situation.

The third hurdle is closely connected with the previous two. It involves the selection of support systems consistent with your assertion to move ahead with your life.

Often, an examination of your life will reveal patterns of interacting in relationships which are unhealthy or less productive than you desire. As you discover how you want to live life, you must also seek to build support for the positive changes you are making.

Again, people who made up your support system prior to the death of your loved one may or may not agree with your new approach to life. They may not always be honest or objective in what they tell you or recommend for you. They may have their own personal agendas as they relate to you. Individuals who have lost a spouse, for example, find that some friends will always see them as part of a "couple" and will never be able to accept the change brought about by the loss. They can also be resistant to other changes, such as the addition of a new spouse or relationship at some later point in time.

However, remember that you are the producer and director of your new life! You are the lead actor! It is up to you to decide who will play the supporting roles in your new life. Provided your new directions are not harmful to you or others, it is imperative that your supporting cast agrees with your new directions. This means that you may have to focus less attention on those who would "keep you in your place," and turn your focus toward those who are capable of helping you move along your new, chosen paths.

You will have to learn to ask for what you want and need. Growth should be your new directive, and support consistent with that growth will be necessary in your work of mourning. Therefore, you must begin to free yourself of hindrances — thoughts, perceptions and people — who would keep you from achieving your goals and begin to rely on support systems consistent with positive change and growth.

The Choice to Begin Rebuilding

The third choice in the Mid-Mourning Phase is to begin rebuilding. An allusion has already been made to the similarities between facing the death of a loved one and facing the devastation of a natural disaster. This allusion may be carried a step further to include deciding what directions to pursue next. Following a storm, the sorting of debris left in its wake and the clean-up involved, comes rebuilding.

Individuals who have faced the aftermath of a natural disaster know the importance of putting a life back together in some really practical ways. They must consider when to rebuild, how to go about it, where to locate or relocate, what resources are available and how they will be used, and what avenues are open through insurance settlements and loans. They may have suffered the loss of personal property and home, as well as business and work. This is an enormous task! Eventually, most people find a way to begin the rebuilding process. They find the strength and vision necessary to dream, plan and start over.

The same is true for you as you face the third choice of the Mid-Mourning Phase of grief. By this point, you will have experienced the devastation of the event, evaluated and sorted through your relationship and life, and will have begun working through the painful realities of life without your loved one. You will have with you those experiences, memories and values which provide comfort and direction and will then be ready to begin rebuilding your life — a new life. You are facing the what, when, where and how questions which face any rebuilding project. The only difference is that you are answering these questions with your life on the line. As you gather all the resources of which you are aware and to which you have access, the need for blueprints and models of what you want to build becomes very clear.

No rebuilding project worth the effort can be done without some sort of planning and testing. It is no different with your life. The choice to begin rebuilding starts with developing blueprints and constructing models of how you envision the end product. The questions of what kind of life you want, what you want to do, where you want to be and how you intend to get there are all part of this process. This choice involves dreaming, projecting into the future and visualizing — the blueprints and the models.

My grandfather was a carpenter — a true craftsman, builder and inventor. He took pride in his work, whether it was the repair of a cabinet door or the construction of a home from the ground up. As a boy, I was amazed at how skilled he was at his work. Sometimes I would catch him sitting in his rocking chair at the end of a day's work, staring off into space. "Grandpop," I would ask, "what are you doing?" His attention would turn to my question and he would say something like, "Oh, I'm just thinking about the house I'm building."

I never fully appreciated that process until I was older. Although I never was able to jump inside his mind, I know that he was dreaming, projecting and visualizing just how to build the house to his specifications. He constantly worked from blueprints and models. He would never hesitate to change or alter a blueprint or plan if what he tried did not produce the intended outcome. He was innovative and a risk taker. He believed in his abilities, his dreams, his product. If he was afraid of failure, he hardly ever let it show. When something did not work out the way he had envisioned, he would go back to the drawing board and start again. He made mistakes and miscalculations at times — he was not perfect. Yet, in each project, he worked at making it match his vision.

For you, the choice to begin rebuilding requires that you, also, draw up blueprints and construct models. It is a time of dreaming and visualizing about what you want your life to be from this point forward. It is a choice to try out new roles and ideas which have emerged as you have reflected on your life. It is a time to begin extending beyond yourself into the world around you — a world very different than it was before. It is a time to risk the new you and your new plans. This is done through conversations with friends and family members, attending and sharing in support groups, and when necessary, making inquiries of other people who can help you realize your plans.

It is also a time in which you may experience some ambivalence because you are not quite through dealing with the past. Guilt for moving on, feelings of betrayed loyalties and the influences of self-perception before the loss can surface at times, causing you to question your directions. Yet, what is most important is that you seek to regain a sense of balance in your life, to integrate the loss into your life and move forward.

Many times, you may find yourself going back to the drawing board, re-working your blueprints and altering your models. You, too, will make mistakes and miscalculations. That is all right! The point is that you will be engaging in active involvement with the world and testing your discoveries and dreams! It can be frightening and invigorating at the same time! I encourage you to dream and try! As you do this, you will discover that you are rebuilding your life and you can feel some satisfaction from your success. You are participating in Good Mourning!

LATE MOURNING — THE CONTINUATION

The Panhandle region of Texas is famous (or infamous, as the case may be) for the tornadoes which sweep through the countryside each spring. Having grown up in that part of the country, it was not unusual for me to be rudely awakened in the middle of the night by high winds, torrential rain, hail, loud, crashing thunder and blinding lightening which momentarily froze the pitch black landscape into eerie snapshots of powerless houses, windblown trees and flying debris. The storm siren would sound and my family would dash for the storm cellar in hope that the threatened tornado would not carry us away before we reached safety. I remember my family, on many occasions, huddling together in the cellar built by my grandfather, wondering what was happening to everything above ground.

Often, after the storm had passed, we would go back into the house and go back to bed. Although I went to bed, I rarely slept the rest of the night. I would lie awake anticipating the dawn — anxious to see how the storm had changed the town and surrounding areas. Would anything be blown away? Had there been a flood at the creek in the park? Had anyone been injured or killed? Would anything be different?

As the dawn crept into my room, I knew that I could begin to explore the aftermath of the storm. Often, I would think that morning would never come, but it always did. I was always so relieved to see the sun begin brightening the sky. I knew that no matter what had happened the night before, I was alive and the storm had passed. I had another day to live, explore and grow.

The beginning of the Late Mourning Phase of grief is much like awaiting the dawn following a night of stormy weather. You have been rudely awakened by the storm of the event and you are terrified because of the devastation around you. You realize that one whom you loved did not make it through the storm and you are left trembling at the prospect of facing the world outside the storm cellar alone.

You think that the dawn will never break. You ponder over how you will go on with your life. You wonder if you will ever be able to live a "normal" life again. You spend time thinking about how life was before the event and how it will be different now. You even begin planning how you will approach getting on with your life. Yet, you are still waiting for the dawn so you can begin to explore your world in earnest.

Eventually, whether suddenly or gradually, you realize that dawn has indeed come and although things are different — you are different — you have the chance to begin living the life you have constructed during the wait. Life does, in fact, go on and you are a part of that life. You have responsibilities to yourself and the world around you. You have opportunities to create something unique through your efforts.

The night is over and the day has come. Now you can begin to explore, grow and experience life as a person who has survived and is determined to live successfully following the loss.

THE CHARACTERISTICS OF LATE MOURNING

*T*he Late Mourning Phase of the grief process focuses on getting on with your life — the continuation of life following the loss. As stated earlier, it is important to remember that the various feelings associated with grief may be experienced at any point in the process of mourning. For example, you may discover that you experience anger or sadness during any phase; however, that anger or sadness may be for different reasons connected with the loss and may vary in intensity in each phase.

As you enter Late Mourning, you will discover that the three characteristics most associated with this phase focus less on feelings of grief and more on attitudes and perceptions as they relate to moving on with your life.

An Attitude of Acceptance

Acceptance of the loss and your situation are key components in your ability to move on with life in a healthy manner; however, the prevailing attitude of acceptance necessary to accomplish this does not come all at once.

Some who work in the field of grief recovery inadvertently communicate that acceptance is something which is achieved — a goal toward which individuals strive. In my thinking, this communicates that acceptance of the loss, your situation, your changed life and accompanying possibilities await you at the end of some magical rainbow. It seems to say that once you reach this "special place," you will experience acceptance.

I tend to disagree with this notion. I do not believe that acceptance is a goal to be attained. On the contrary, acceptance is the motivating force which can help you get through the process of mourning. It is the daily process of accepting the reality of your situation through healthy expressions of your grief.

It is the affirmation of your personhood, your life and your possibilities through demonstrations of lessons learned and insights gained.

Acceptance is gradual — a process which must be worked each day. You will not suddenly "arrive" at the destination of acceptance and be "okay." You will work at it each and every day and develop a prevailing attitude of acceptance which may be more readily transferred as you deal with loss issues in other areas of your life.

Many physicians and nurses recognize the importance of daily work with acceptance and affirmation in the healing of abdominal surgery patients. Individuals who have experienced abdominal surgery are encouraged to begin walking soon after the surgery in order to facilitate timely healing. Although it is difficult in the beginning, the patients discover that by walking, they are better able to accept their situation and affirm their abilities to do for themselves.

Integration of the Loss into Your Life-Scheme

A second characteristic is that of integration of the loss into your life-scheme. As you work at the daily process of acceptance and affirmation, you will be integrating the loss into your life as well. Integration is essential for healthy recovery in that it allows you to be in touch with your own pain associated with loss and with the pain of other individuals who find themselves in similar circumstances. One who has fully integrated loss through the process of acceptance and affirmation may be better able to grieve future personal losses and assist others as they grieve losses as well.

The prevailing attitude of acceptance and the integration of your loss, however, does not mean that you are immune to surges of grief feelings at times. An individual who has fully integrated loss is still likely to be swept by feelings of grief on occasion. This experience is common and to be expected. Once you have been sensitized to the pain of loss, it is difficult to escape its effects. You may find yourself being swept momentarily with feelings of sadness or longing or fear in certain situations. There may be various triggers causing these feelings to surface. Do not be afraid of them. Holidays, places or activities special to you and/or your loved one, smells, sounds, another person's loss, etc. — all of these can serve as triggers for these momentary surges of grief. It is perfectly all right to experience these surges of grief. In fact, these surges can serve to keep you aware of your progress and may happen from time to time throughout the rest of your life.

The key to remember is that, at this point, you will no longer be dominated by grief — you will have come to the place where you will be comfortable with your grief as well as the grief of others. This freedom from being dominated by grief may enable you to encounter the third characteristic of the Late Mourning Phase.

Emergence of a Present-Tense Focus

The third characteristic associated with the Late Mourning Phase of the grief process is that of the emergence of a present-tense focus. Up to this point, much of your time and energy will most likely have been spent reflecting on the past and wondering about the future. You may have looked back on your life with your loved one with mixed feelings of guilt, anger, regret, relief, joy, pride or longing. You may have projected yourself into the future, experiencing fear, uncertainty, anticipation, anxiety or excitement— another set of mixed feelings!

As you move into this new phase, you may begin to realize that you are ready to realistically face your life in the "here and now." You may realize that the past cannot be changed or altered — only your perceptions of it can be — and that the future is yet to be. You may realize more than ever before that there are no guarantees and that your tomorrows may never come. You may even recognize just how precious life is and come to value your place in it in a way you never have. In this phase, you experience an emerging focus on the present-tense.

In the present-tense focus, you may find yourself with a heightened sense of the immediate — not wanting to let things pass you by. You may be more aware of sights, sounds, beauty, people, relationships and the parts they play in your life. You will focus on the things which make up your life at that point — the more immediate concerns facing you. As you continue to accept, affirm and integrate the loss into your life, you will be able to spend more of your emotional, mental, physical and spiritual energy on today. You will realize that today is the only day you are guaranteed and that anything you want to do must be accomplished right now.

I do not mean that you must attempt to do everything all at once, but you will find yourself working within the framework of today to accomplish the goals you have set. You will see the need for balance and priorities in your life and seek those activities and people which will assist you in creating them.

Anything you do with your life will be done in all of its "todays" — never in its yesterdays or tomorrows. You will discover how to learn and draw from the past and dream and plan for the future as you live in the "here and now."

THE CHALLENGES OF
LATE MOURNING

*I*n the Late Mourning Phase, you will be ready to truly face the world as the new person you will have become and will still be in the process of becoming as a result of your loss.

You will be, as it were, a butterfly emerging from your cocoon. In the early going, you will be very vulnerable and will need to discover how to take care of yourself, very much like a caterpillar. You may feel in need of protection and support. You will need to find healthy ways to begin the grieving process. This, again, is the phase of Early Mourning.

Fairly soon after the loss and your early grieving, you will be ready to move into the Mid-Mourning phase, which may be likened to the caterpillar's construction of the cocoon. In much the same manner that the butterfly-to-be goes through a metamorphosis unseen by human eyes, individuals begin the process of reflection, change, integration and healing — much of which is done in the private moments of time, thoughts and feelings. This is the transition phase of grief work. As those who have gone through the transition know, this process can be grueling and excruciatingly painful at times and cannot be rushed.

Once you create the structure of what you want to become, you will begin the process of emerging from the cocoon — the continuation of your life — the Late Mourning Phase of your grief. However painless and effortless you might like this emergence to be, there will still be effort and struggle. Although the butterfly has all the appearances of a creature ready to fly, this new creation must struggle and push and work to free itself from the cocoon which has been its home for a period of time. This process is necessary, for if the butterfly remains in the cocoon, it will die. Likewise, if the butterfly receives too much assistance in emerging, it will not have the strength to live as intended — it must emerge from the cocoon on its own or perish.

This emergence to continuation has three challenges which must be faced with courage. During this phase you will be challenged to Re-define Closure, Work on a Life Plan and Prepare for Setbacks.

Re-define Closure

Closure is defined as a closing or shutting up — a conclusion. These definitions tend to carry with them the picture of having something tied up neatly in a package — a package with definite boundaries and parameters. Human beings tend to seek the kind of closure on relationships and events consistent with the definitions above.

These definitions may sometimes cause you to believe that all experiences you face may be tied up in packages, never to be unwrapped again. This type of belief system may set you up for disappointment and disillusionment.

Unfortunately, relationships and events such as the loss of a loved one are not easily tied up in packages, and the conclusions are not always as clear-cut as you might desire them to be. With that in mind, it is necessary to re-define closure to better facilitate your continuation with life following loss.

Instead of visualizing closure as tying things up in packages, it may be beneficial to view your experiences as being placed in glass test tubes. There are two advantages to viewing closure in this way. First is the realization that experiences, such as the loss of a loved one, have long-term effects on your life and you will be faced with questions about them at various times throughout your life.

Often, these questions and feelings associated with a particular experience will bubble up in your conscious thoughts at random or as a result of certain triggers. It is as if the feelings associated with the experience you have placed in a particular test tube have taken themselves off the rack and jumped on the Bunson Burner and are demanding your attention. This can be rather disconcerting if you view feelings and experiences as things never to be dealt with again once they have been wrapped up.

Often, the feelings associated with experiences simply need to be acknowledged, and any original decisions need only to be reaffirmed. If you view closure as a test tube, you will not be surprised when thoughts, feelings or experiences bubble up in your mind. You can expect that they will bubble up from time to time and can be somewhat prepared for them. You will be able to ask questions such as, "Has anything changed since I last thought about this situation?" or "Do I need to investigate the situation further at this point?" This attitude allows you to tell yourself what it is you want or need to do with the situation at the time it comes up. If you do not need to do anything with the thought, feeling or situation, you may simply acknowledge it and move on. If, on the other hand, you need to re-evaluate the situation or feeling and add any new insight, you have the opportunity to do so.

The second advantage to viewing closure as a test tube lies in the fact that there will be times when new information or insights will become available to you through the process of growth and investigation.

If you view closure as a test tube, you will be able to re-call, at will, an event or experience or any feeling connected with it. You then will be able to determine whether the new information alters your perceptions or decisions connected to the experience, and you will be able to take the appropriate action to incorporate the new information into your life framework.

If the new information or insight does not affect the original closure of the experience, you have not lost anything at all by reviewing it.

In short, to re-define closure in the manner described is to define it as an ongoing process which may facilitate continued personal growth rather than a rigid box with well-defined limits which are resistant to exploration. This re-definition may help you face the winds of life like a willow tree which has the ability to bend and move with the flow, rather than a rigid oak tree which resists the wind.

In this life, only the flexible survive and continue to grow!

Work on a Life-Plan

The importance of developing a life-plan during this phase of your mourning process cannot be underestimated. The concept of continuation carries with it the ideas of stability and survival. You are a survivor — you will create a certain sense of stability in your life as you move through the process of mourning.

The challenge of developing a life-plan proceeds naturally from this sense of being a survivor and the stability you will create. You will have already participated in the process of forming a tentative direction for your life during the Mid-Mourning Phase of the process by deciding to assert yourself and begin rebuilding. You will have created and tried various blueprints and models, seeking to find a comfortable direction in which to go. Finally, then, will be the time for you to develop those dreams and models into a more formalized life-plan. This life-plan may be best described as the overall goal or dream for your life.

I remember the first time I was confronted with the contemplation of my life-plan following my wife Christy's death. I was visiting with my friend and life insurance agent at his office when the following exchange took place. He said, "I would ask, 'what are you going to do now,' but that is not the question I want to ask. Instead, I want to ask, 'What do you want to do now?'"

No one had ever asked me that question in exactly the same manner before. I was quiet for a moment and, before I really knew what was happening, I responded, "I want to write, teach and speak." That seminal statement became the framework around which I began to structure both my grief work and my eventual life-plan.

I knew that for my life to be of use and worth to myself, my daughter and anyone else who entered my life, I would have to involve myself in healthy grief work. I knew that if I wanted my writing, teaching and speaking to contribute to the well-being of others, it would be necessary for me to learn how to mourn my loss in healthy and effective ways. Obviously, my life-plan grew and became more all-encompassing to include relationships and remarriage, but the important point here is that I began to work with a life-plan.

The development of a life-plan involves the following distinct aspects: your overall dream or goal, your statement of purpose or intent, your strategy or action steps, and your measure of progress.

Step One asks: What do you want to do?

The first step in beginning to pursue your overall dream or goal involves the question my friend asked me. I ask you the same question. What do you want to do? As you work on this part of your life-plan, it will be helpful for you to verbalize your thoughts to others who have an interest in you and an ability to be objective about your statements. It may also be helpful for you to write down your dreams and goals to get a handle on what it is you really do want to do, become, create, have and/or enjoy. You might begin by completing the following statement: "I want to . . ." This may help you formulate your thoughts into the beginnings of your life-plan.

Step Two asks: What are the parts of your goal?

The second step involves breaking your overall goal down into its various parts. In my experience, I discovered that to teach, I had to go back to school to obtain a teaching certificate. This became one of my statements of purpose or intent. It went something like this: "To be able to teach, I must enroll in college and meet the requirements for teaching certification." I went through this process with each part of my overall dream or goal. For me, this part of the process was exciting and challenging. As you begin to work on your life-plan, you may find this experience an exciting challenge as well.

In some cases, however, rather than breaking down a goal, you may decide to redefine the plan altogether. This, too, is an important part of the process. As you move ahead, you will continue to clarify, re-evaluate and update your plans and how you will achieve them.

Step Three asks: What strategy or action steps will you take?

The third step requires you to specify the strategy or action steps which will help you accomplish each statement of purpose or intent. This becomes the "how" for each statement.

Again, following the example already mentioned, I found that I had to investigate the entrance requirements to the university, any deficiencies I had to make up in my course work, the requirements for state certification beyond the coursework, and the time involved before I would be able to complete the entire project. This information became part of my strategy to be able to teach. In all, I found that my certification could be accomplished in one year.

In your own life, consider the steps you will need to take to make your statement of purpose a reality. How much time or money will it require? What other resources or support do you need to accomplish your purpose?

This statement of purpose does not necessarily have to be written down, but it will help you focus your efforts to do so.

Step Four asks: How will you measure your progress?

The fourth and final step in the development of your life-plan focuses on measuring your progress.

Basically, this step involves keeping track of your progress as you work your life-plan. It causes you to ask such questions as: "How will I know whether I have attained this particular part of my plan? What do I need to do differently to reach my goal? How does my strategy need to be altered?"

This step will cause you to check your progress and remind you that you are in control of your responses and choices as you move ahead.

Rarely will a particular statement of purpose be attained without some degree of re-evaluation and change. The temptation here will be to ask "why" when you meet resistance to your goals. A common problem with the "why" question, as it relates to challenges encountered while working on your goal, is that there is a tendency to try to place blame on someone or something else for the challenge or problem encountered.

Instead, it is better to ask, "What can I do differently, or change, to attain my goal?" This causes you to think in terms of options and possibilities, rather than in rigid, linear terms of blame when it comes to meeting your goals — a set-up for failure.

The important point to remember is that you are constantly checking your progress — you are in control of how you work your plan.

Prepare For Setbacks

Surprises can either be fun and exciting or frustrating and disappointing. Depending on your experiences with surprises, you may either welcome them or shy away from them.

Surprises in the form of setbacks can be very disappointing and disheartening. It would be wonderful if the world would welcome, with open arms, your efforts to rebuild your life following your loss, but that will not always be the case. That is why it is imperative that you face the challenge of preparing for setbacks, for they will inevitably come.

Sometimes these setbacks will come from friends and family members who make statements — whether intentional or unintentional — which discourage your efforts to rebuild. Other times, the setbacks can come from within as you deal with thoughts, attitudes and feelings which have been debilitating to you in other situations. Still other setbacks have their origins in bureaucratic rules and regulations or natural circumstances. These setbacks can affect you emotionally, mentally, spiritually and physically, depending on the nature of the source.

The key to handling setbacks lies in being prepared for their occurrence. I am not saying that you must be able to anticipate each and every setback. Rather, you will do yourself a favor to accept the fact that they will happen. This acceptance of the reality of living may keep you from feeling so devastated when they do come. Because you are successfully working through your loss now, you will be better prepared to face the setbacks ahead as you continue to live.

THE CHOICES OF LATE MOURNING

*T*he choices associated with the Late Mourning Phase of your grief may be classified as choices of extension and expansion. These are appropriate qualifiers in that they convey growth, adventure, change and risk. Nothing could better describe the choices of this phase.

In this phase, you are in the midst of continuing on with your life. When you have worked diligently at learning how to mourn in healthy ways, you will be more prepared for this task. Yet, even though you will be better prepared, you may still feel a little anxious about your future — you will not know what awaits you as you venture forward.

I am reminded of a scene from the movie "Far and Away," where hundreds of people are lined up at the starting line awaiting the signal to begin their dash for "free land" on which to begin building or rebuilding their dreams. Each individual, each family, had pinned hopes on being able to find, claim and hold on to prime real estate — the stuff of which dreams are made. When the shot rang out over the plains setting the hopefuls on their way, the tension, anxiety and excitement exploded in a rush of horses' hooves, shouts and frantic activity. Dust billowed, hats flew, women hung on to their wagons white-knuckled, and children clung to each other for dear life as they bounced along in the back of buckboards and wagons — all seeking the same goal — a new life filled with promise and contentment.

You, too, will be poised at a similar starting line. As you grasp the characteristics of this phase and understand the challenges which await you, you may realize that the choices which lie ahead are not for the faint-hearted. These choices will require work, perseverance and endurance on your part. The territory before you is wild, unexplored and full of possibility! It is up to you to find, claim and hold on to the things which will provide you a full and meaningful life. It will be difficult at times, but the rewards can be so wonderful!

As you move into this territory, the choices you will face can provide you with the tools necessary to make life what you want it to be. In the Late Mourning Phase, you will be asked to choose to Engage Opposition, to Keep Going and to Share Yourself With Others.

The Choice To Engage Opposition

This first choice relates specifically to the challenge of being prepared for setbacks in your attempts to rebuild your life. The fact of the matter is that you will encounter resistance and setbacks as you move ahead — that is a given! You have already learned that being prepared for these experiences can help you mobilize your resources when faced with opposition. At this point, then, you must choose to engage the opposition you will face in order to win the struggle.

The choice here may be likened to the scenario played out in the life of a professional athlete. Each week, the athlete must prepare for the upcoming contest. The athlete knows that he or she will face opposition equally prepared and determined. The athlete will have a game plan designed to bring victory, complete with alternative plans if the original does not work as intended.

Finally, the day of the contest arrives, and the athlete must step into the fray. The thrill, the anticipation, the anxiety, the uncertainty cause adrenaline to flow, and only action will alleviate the tension which has built up. With all this in mind, can you imagine the athlete — as well prepared as possible, goals and plans in place, dressed for the contest — deciding to stand on the side-line and choosing to not go into the game? That is almost unthinkable, isn't it? Not only would the fans wonder what could have happened had the athlete competed in the event, the athlete, too, would probably wonder the same thing.

Fear, uncertainty or even lack of confidence could all cause the athlete to decline participation, but the fact of the matter is that he or she has the choice of facing or not facing the opposition.

At this point in the process, you will be faced with a similar scenario. You will be as well prepared as you can be, you will have your goals and plans in place, you will be ready to enter the game to win. The choice you will face is, do you engage the opposition or not?

Remember, opposition to your progress and success is a given — that is just the way life operates. You will never know how your plans will work unless you engage the opposition as it comes at you. There will be a certain amount of fear, anxiety and questioning of your abilities as you move forward — you will never be able to determine how your life will turn out if you stand on the side-line and observe. You do not have a choice as to what kinds of situations life will deal you, but you will have a choice as to how you respond to those situations.

A choice to engage opposition is a choice to involve yourself in life. Nothing can be as frightening and rewarding at the same time. Remember, you will not be alone in this choice. You will have built a support team of people around you who believe in change, growth and you. Although your team will stand ready, only you can fill the slot labeled with your name. I encourage you to Engage the Opposition!

The Choice to Keep Going

Endurance, perseverance and determination come to mind when thinking about the second choice of the Late Mourning Phase of the grief process. At this point, you must choose to Keep Going. The process to which this choice refers is the need to continue making choices as you move ahead with your life. This is likely not the first loss you will have ever experienced in your life, and it will not be the last. It is likely that this loss has caused past losses to come to the surface, some of which may not have been fully mourned. You may have found yourself grieving several of these losses at the same time — all triggered by this most recent one. The point is that as you choose to keep making choices, you will gain wisdom for living. You will learn to face whatever comes next in your life.

To keep going, it will be essential that you "Learn to Do the Next Thing" and "Learn to Go the Distance." Let's explore each in more detail.

Learning to Do the Next Thing

I remember two things happening to me on the morning my wife Christy died. The doctor came into the waiting room, looked at me and said, "Mr. Hundley, I am sorry to tell you this, but your wife is dead." Those words shook me to the very core of my being. I collapsed on the floor and wept — the disbelief, anger, bitterness, frustration, confusion and fear pouring out of my soul with the tears which streamed down my face. What would I do?

Almost before I knew what was happening, a voice from inside me said, "Mark, there are lots of people here, and they don't know what to say and they don't know what to do. There are lots of decisions to be made, and the only one who can make these decisions is you, so get up and start making them now!" I responded to this internal prompting, rose to sit on the couch in the waiting room and faced the doctor.

As I sat there, my thoughts raced back to the major points from a sermon I heard a college pastor preach back in 1974, titled "In the Meantime." He referred to life's difficulties and interruptions as "meantimes," and facing the death of a loved one is truly a "meantime" in life. He outlined three things to do when life's meantimes intrude on our existence. He said that we must Lean Heavily on God, Lean Heavily on our Family and Friends, and Do the Next Thing.

To illustrate the third point, he said, "If you happen to be washing the dishes, and your meantime comes and you have to leave the dishes to take care of the situation — as soon as you can, go back and finish washing the dishes."

Doing the next thing, learning to work at life and living, are a part of this choice to keep going — a choice which demands marathon-type resolve.

Learning to Go the Distance

I have run two 26.2 mile marathon races in my life. I remember the first time I contemplated participating in such a race. I could not envision finishing that long a distance — it was difficult enough to run two miles without stopping. Nevertheless, I started the process of training and spent many long hours running in all types of weather just to get ready.

After several months of training, the day of my first marathon came. I was excited and apprehensive at the same time. I decided that I would finish the distance no matter what.

Things were going well through 20 miles when I suddenly developed cramps in my calves. The pain was so great at times that I wanted to stop and not finish the race at all. I later discovered that I had suffered a stress fracture in my left tibia in addition to the muscle cramps. Fortunately, two young friends also running had volunteered to meet me at mile 18 to ensure that I finished the race. I was certainly glad they were there! They stopped with me, we massaged the cramps out and continued. I did make it through the final 6 miles, and the experience was incredible! In that one race, I learned a tremendous lesson about getting on with life following loss.

It became clear to me that the marathon was a metaphor of life. Goals, dreams, plans, effort, pain, setbacks, temptations to quit, self-doubt, feelings of optimism, accomplishment and satisfaction at completion — all of these experiences were mine in the time it took me to run the course. The same may be said for living life following loss. The choice to keep going is the choice to go the distance — calling upon all the resources available to you while you run the race. Once you have come this far, KEEP GOING!

The Choice to Share Yourself With Others

I have often wondered what would have happened if Jonas Salk had decided not to share the information he discovered about fighting polio, or how my life would be different today if Louis Pasteur had kept his discoveries silent. Where would I be today if Albert Einstein had given up experimenting and exploring after many failures? I am not sure these questions can be answered completely, but I do believe that life would be quite different if they had not shared their discoveries.

You will be in very much the same situation in the Late Mourning Phase. You will have traveled far in your journey through the land of mourning and will have gathered great insights and wisdom. The path will have been long, grueling and sometimes tedious.

You will have faced many obstacles and will have successfully maneuvered your way through treacherous waters. You will have been through forests of despair, deserts of loneliness, valleys of fear and over mountains of doubt. At times, you will have found meadows of rest and springs of rejuvenation. You will have contemplated your future beside soothing reflection ponds. You will have found refuge in quiet caves of thought. You will have looked out over the plains of possibility and dreamed of your future. You will have participated in Good Mourning! It will then be time to face the choice to share yourself with others.

Few experiences in life can be as anxiety-producing or as rewarding as sharing your life and experiences with others. On one hand, you really cannot determine how people will respond to your openness and honesty. You see, individuals like you have a story to tell — a story which can cause some to be encouraged and inspired while, at the same time, can cause others to feel resentful and bitter. On the other hand, you are living in a society which tends to try to deny death and mourning. One who has successfully negotiated the tasks of mourning may cause the status quo to be questioned.

With these things in mind, choosing to share yourself with others is still one of the best ways to both keep yourself on track to healthy living and provide a model of success and encouragement to those with whom you have contact who face death and loss. One of the ways you can achieve and maintain emotional and mental health is by extending yourself beyond yourself into the lives of others.

Once you have reached this phase of mourning, you will truly have something of substance to share with other hurting individuals. You will understand the process through which they are going. You can identify with the struggles they are facing. You can empathize with their life experiences. You can be a wealth of information and support.

I encourage you to extend yourself beyond yourself and share your life with those suffering the pain of loss. Not only will you feel more fulfilled, you will help make the world a place where it is safe to feel and express feelings. You will be a pioneer in the field of healing — healing from the pain of grief. Share yourself with others!

Getting Started on the Work of Good Mourning

Your Support System

When you reach this fourth section of the book — and have progressed to this point in your grief work — you will have built a solid foundation for the end of your journey down the path of Good Mourning. The time for action will be at hand, and your future will rest with you alone. While only you can decide where your life goes from here, remember that you can still benefit from the assistance of individuals, groups, organizations, support systems and other resources.

My experience has been that people tend to work in healthier ways and integrate loss more effectively when assistance from others and a variety of resources are readily available. These resources form the basis of a positive support network so necessary as you work through your loss. The network consists of three support systems, which focus on clarifying how you derive meaning from life through your beliefs and values, how you access support from those around you, and how you draw upon your own personal strengths and abilities.

Support From Beliefs and Values

As you search for purpose and meaning in life, your beliefs and values will take on new importance. You may find yourself questioning and re-evaluating long-held beliefs and values. This process is very common, and I encourage you to explore it. Whether your values include a belief in God or some higher power, a pursuit of humanitarian activities, or a search for individual discovery and growth, I urge you to involve yourself in strengthening this support system.

You may begin by attending the next meeting of an organization to which you belong or would like to belong, or by making an appointment with your minister, priest or rabbi to discuss opportunities for growth and service. You might consider keeping a journal of how you are finding new purpose in life through the pursuit of your values and beliefs.

You might also start reading books to help strengthen your values and beliefs. Participation in various seminars or workshops can also foster growth, especially those focusing on values clarification or personal development.

Whatever you do, I encourage you to involve yourself in the pursuit of your personal faith and values. This pursuit can contribute to expressions of healthy grief and can assist in your recovery and continuation.

Support From Those Around You

The support you can receive from friends, family members and your community is immeasurable! Not only can they function as a source of moral and social support, but they can also serve you in very practical ways.

To benefit, you must learn how to effectively access these resources as they exist in your community. Friends, family members, clergy, professional counselors and therapists, attorneys, physicians, churches, synagogues and temples, support groups, service organizations, financial advisors, insurance agents, funeral directors, colleges and universities, health and fitness clubs, hospitals, the YMCA and YWCA — all of these and many more make up potential resources of support from those around you. I encourage you to begin expanding this support system to give yourself even more options as you progress.

Support From Within

In the midst of this difficult situation, you cannot afford to sit back and passively wait for something to happen to make you better or for someone to do for you the things only you have the capacity to do for yourself. The success you have in your recovery and continuation is up to you. It is a matter of believing in yourself and your personal resources as you move forward.

As you draw on the support from your own strengths and abilities, you may discover that you are able to do a better job of establishing your long-term goals. You may also find yourself able to create a more unified philosophy of life, freeing you to make choices in the midst of uncertainty. Both of these discoveries may help you gain confidence in your abilities and strengths as you progress.

Take Practical Steps

The work of Good Mourning requires you to take practical steps toward your recovery. At the end of this book, you will find four appendices containing guidelines and resources to help you take those steps.

Appendix A is a checklist of contacts which need to be made in the early part of your mourning experience. These contacts relate to the settlement of estate matters, insurance matters, Social Security and the like. This section can be used as a guide to help you settle the affairs of your loved one.

Appendix B is a list of books and other written resources available to assist you and your family in dealing with the grief process. Listings are divided according to the specific challenges facing children, adolescents and adults. As you finish this book, you may want to find other support books as well, and develop your own personal library based on your needs and the needs of your family. I hope this book will be just the beginning of your written resource collection as you begin a healthy journey to recovery.

Appendix C contains a list of national self-help and support organizations related to specific types of loss. You may be able to use this list as a beginning point to determine which support groups and organizations exist in your particular area of the country. As you find the groups which have chapters in your area, you may have an easier time becoming involved in appropriate support activities.

Appendix D is designed to help you outline important resources to call on, and to assist you in setting goals for expanding these resources in the future. This section consists of personal worksheets to help you organize the necessary contacts to be made and the community support organizations or individuals to be added to your network. I encourage you to sit down with a trusted friend, advisor or family member to gain additional input as you complete these worksheets.

Closing Thoughts

The death of a loved one is life's most crushing blow. You have demonstrated your desire to grieve this loss and move on in a healthy manner by reading this book. I believe that you have the resources to successfully work through this painful and difficult time in your life and emerge a stronger person. It will not come easily — you will have to work at it; however, you are not alone. There are many individuals and resources available to assist you.

I hope the information presented in this book has been helpful and that you will refer to it over and again as you work through your grief. In summary, I would like to leave you with the following thoughts:

1. Life can be good! — Your life is and will be different, but different does not have to mean worse. You can have a meaningful and productive life despite your loss. Begin now to dream about what your good life can be. Make the dream your life goal.

2. People do create good lives! — You are responsible for how you respond to what happens in your life. Once you have created the goals for your good life, begin formulating a plan. Form some very specific and measurable

steps to help accomplish your goal. Then work toward your goal and live your dream each day!

3. You are the key! — If you find that things are not working according to your plan, trust yourself and your abilities enough to shift gears and make some changes in your approach. Try never to ask "Why" when your plan does not work. Instead, ask, "What can I do differently to accomplish what I want?" As you keep this attitude, you may find others more willing to assist you in moving ahead.

Awaken To Good Mourning!

Finding healthy and useful ways to mourn the loss of friends or loved ones is difficult work. Throughout my professional life, I have always found tremendous challenge and comfort in helping those facing the pain of loss.

Following my wife Christy's death, I was even more aware of how important it is to have tools and resources available to help grieving individuals and families. It was for this reason that "Awaken to Good Mourning" was written.

The information I have shared comes from my own journey through loss and mourning. As a result of my experiences, I am more empathetic toward people than I have ever been, and, at the same time, more hopeful that healthy grief work and recovery can be realities. There are so many restrictions placed on grieving individuals by society, family, friends and self — the restrictions which cause bad mourning. Too many people become stuck in bad mourning experiences — that's why I want you, and others like you, to realize that there can be Good Mourning as well.

As I reflect today on my life so far, I can truly say that I am thankful I awakened to Good Mourning. I now have a new life, a new career, a new wife and a different kind of family. I have integrated the loss into my life.

Have I forgotten my previous life? No! Not at all! I have been able to take all the positives from my past, merge them with the experiences of the present and work toward a future with hope and fulfillment.

I am learning the power of living in the present tense. I know the benefits of Good Mourning! It has worked for me, and it can work for you, too.

Take the challenge life has presented and make it positive. Today, I urge you to raise the blinds of your eyes, open the windows of your soul and AWAKEN TO GOOD MOURNING!

APPENDIX A:

IMPORTANT CONTACTS

During this early mourning stage, you will find yourself in a state of flux. This can be a very strange and frightening time in your life. It is important to make sure that certain initial contacts are made. If you have already made the contacts discussed below, good for you! If you have yet to make these contacts, then you will want to be sure to do so as soon as possible. If you feel that you are unable to make these calls alone, find a trusted, caring and sympathetic friend or relative to assist. Making these contacts and the necessary decisions which accompany them may open the door for you to begin mourning your loss in a healthy way. They may also provide assistance as you continue on with your life from this point forward.

Contact An Attorney

The primary purpose of making legal contact is to obtain advice on such matters as recording property deeds, taking care of any stocks or bonds your loved one may have owned, determining the disposition of any savings accounts, the conservation or disbursement of the assets of the estate of your loved one, disposition of any business assets, the drawing up of a will for the surviving widow, widower, or other family members, and other similar issues as they relate to your individual situation.

If you do not have a trusted family attorney, the local bar association can assist you with referrals. Friends and family members can also be an important source of referral.

If your loved one had a will, obtain a copy of it as soon as possible. Once the will has been located, take it to your attorney so that he or she can begin filing the necessary legal documents for the probate process. Probate does not have to take a tremendously long time, although each case will vary in complexity. Your attorney will walk you through the process as painlessly as possible. Once the will has been processed, you may distribute the estate to the beneficiaries as specified in the will.

If your loved one had no will, it is still very important for you to contact an attorney because the disposition of the estate can become a more complicated process. From the appointment by the court of an administrator of the estate to the estate's final distribution, competent legal counsel is vital. Whether the estate is large or small, covered by a will or not covered, it is important to contact an attorney so that all legal matters can be handled properly. This course of action may ultimately provide you with some peace of mind, allowing you to focus attention on the process of mourning your loss.

Look For Important Papers

Often, individuals will have prepared a list of where all important papers are kept. If this was the case with your loved one, you are fortunate in that the search will not be as difficult. If your loved one did not have a prepared list, then you must make a thorough search for the papers. Places you might want to look are: safe-deposit boxes, briefcases, home and office desks, strongboxes, safes, lockers, shoe boxes, cedar chests, file cabinets, etc.

Be on the lookout for the following: life insurance, disability income, accident and sickness policies; business agreements; notes receivable and payable; securities certificates; bankbooks; deeds to real estate; property lease agreements; wills and/or codicils to wills; copies of recent income tax returns; W-2 forms and other similar records of earnings; your loved one's Social Security number; birth and marriage certificates; military discharge papers and Veterans Administration claim number; automobile registration certificates; installment payment books; certificates of membership in professional organizations, etc.

A word of CAUTION is in order here: Do not discard any official-looking documents! Everything you find could have some potential importance in settling the affairs of your loved one.

Obtain Multiple Copies Of The Death Certificate

Making sure that you have an adequate number of copies of the death certificate is important because the death certificate is the basic document with which you will be working as you settle the estate of your loved one and make any claims to benefits which are rightfully yours. You will need several copies in order to establish claims on life insurance policies, veterans benefits and Social Security benefits. You may also be required to present copies to credit card companies to make claims for credit life insurance on accounts or to have your loved one's name removed from accounts. Often, your funeral director can secure certified copies of the certificate for you. If this is not the case, you may obtain copies for a nominal fee from the office of the clerk or registrar in the town, village, city or county in which your loved one lived. Remember that a photocopy will not be adequate because it does not bear the raised registrar's or clerk's seal which verifies the document as valid and legal.

Contact Your Life Insurance Agent Or Home Office

Generally, life insurance companies require only a statement of claim and a death certificate or statement from the attending physician in order to establish proof of your claim. However, life insurance companies do reserve the right to request additional information or proof if deemed necessary in a given situation.

All life insurance claims should include the following information:
- Policy number(s) and face amount(s).
- Your loved one's full name and address.
- The occupation of your loved one and the date he or she last worked (if applicable).

- Your loved one's date and place of birth, and the source from which this information was obtained (usually the birth certificate or official hospital record).
- The date, place and cause of death (taken from the death certificate).
- The claimant's or beneficiary's name, age, address and Social Security number.

The following list details some additional information your insurance company might require for a claim on any insurance policy held in the name of your loved one:

1. You might be asked to disclose the date when your loved one's health first began to deteriorate, if an illness was connected with the death.
2. If the death occurred strictly from bodily injuries, you might need to indicate whether the injuries and death were the result of accident, suicide or homicide.
3. You might be asked to provide the insurance company with the name and address of each physician who treated your loved one during the five years prior to the death.
4. You might also be asked to verify who was in possession of the policy at the time of death.
5. If you or other beneficiaries elect to receive payment of the benefit through one of the optional payment plans, you will need to indicate which payment option has been elected. (More information on payment plans, and how they work, is provided in the following section, "Options for Payment of the Benefit," pages 93-94.)
6. You may be asked to provide the name of the executor or administrator, if one is to be appointed.
7. You may be asked to provide information concerning any other life insurance policies which may have been in effect on your loved one at the time of death — indicating company, face amount and date.

Options For Payment Of The Benefit

Life insurance proceeds are generally intended to provide a sense of security and continuity for the beneficiary. After you receive the benefits of the policy, you will have to decide what you want to do with them. Unfortunately, this comes at a time when you are probably the least able or prepared to make such decisions. You may face an additional problem if the settlement is a much larger sum of money than you are accustomed to handling. You might feel guilty about receiving the money from an insurance settlement and feel an urge to spend the money as quickly as possible. You may also not be aware of how your loved one planned for the money to be used to support you in case something happened to him or her.

The best advice in a situation where life insurance proceeds are involved is that you make no decisions under duress or pressure. Give yourself time to contemplate how your life has changed and what you need to do now to secure your future. You will need time to counsel with your financial advisors and evaluate your changed financial situation.

All insurance companies have a variety of settlement options available. Although the programs may vary slightly from company to company, they are basically the same. The common settlement options fall into the following general categories:

1. Interest Only — In this option, the principal amount of the settlement remains with the insurance company and the interest is paid periodically to you or another beneficiary. Usually, provisions can be made to have the right to unlimited withdrawal of funds at any time.

2. Life Income or Annuity — In this option, the company will guarantee to pay you or other beneficiaries a pre-determined amount on a set date for the lifetime of the beneficiary/beneficiaries.

3. Fixed Installments — This option provides for payment of benefits according to your needs or the needs of other designated beneficiaries

in agreed-upon amounts over an agreed-upon time period. You or other designated beneficiaries determine the amount of each payment and the duration of payments. This arrangement is similar to a schedule of regular paychecks.

4. Access or Interest-bearing Checking — In this payment option, the company places the benefits in an account on which checks may be written by you or other designated beneficiaries on an as-needed basis. There is generally a minimum balance which must be maintained and a minimum amount for each check written. In most cases, settlements of $10,000 or more will be placed in an account of this type until a final determination of a payment option has been made. Settlements of $10,000 or less will usually be paid in a lump sum payment. If you desire another type of payment option, should your settlement fall below $10,000, you must speak with your agent about any additional options open to you.

Settlement options can be a valuable tool. Consider each option carefully, and be sure to ask the advice of your agent or other financial advisor(s). They are capable of assisting you in evaluating your needs and coming up with a plan to best suit your situation.

Contact The Social Security Office

This can be one of the most important contacts of all. There is a lump sum death benefit of $255 for which you may be eligible, in addition to long-term benefits payable to you or other family members. REMEMBER: Social Security benefits are not automatic — you must apply for them. You might want to consider making an appointment with the nearest Social Security office before going so they can begin reviewing your loved one's records. You may be able to save additional time when applying for these benefits by taking the

following information with you to the Social Security office:
1. Proof of death (death certificate).
2. Your loved one's Social Security number.
3. The approximate earnings of your loved one in the year in which the death occurred and the name of the employer. A record of the earnings of your loved one in the year prior to the death is also suggested.
4. A copy of the marriage certificate (if the deceased was your spouse).
5. The Social Security numbers of the surviving spouse and/or any dependent children.
6. Proof of age of the surviving spouse and of any dependent children who are under the age of 23.

Railroad Workers' Benefits

If your loved one worked for the railroads for 10 or more years, then Railroad Retirement rather than Social Security will provide the benefits. The Social Security Administration is equipped to provide you with the information necessary to apply for the benefits under the Railroad Retirement Act.

Civil Service Benefits

If the deceased was your spouse at the time of death and he or she died in service after at least 18 months on the job, then you are entitled to a survivor's annuity, provided you were either married at least two years before the death or are the father or mother of children by the marriage. Additional variables may apply to your individual situation. It is best to make contact with the U.S. Office of Personnel Management for further details and information.

Applications for benefits, along with a certified copy of the death certificate, may be filed at:

U.S. Office of Personnel Management
Employee Service and Record Center
Boyers, PA 16017
ATTENTION: Death Claims

If additional information is required to properly file a claim for benefits, you will be notified upon receipt of the claim application.

Veterans Benefits

If your loved one was a veteran, a variety of benefits may be rightfully yours — benefits ranging from funds which may applied toward funeral expenses, an American flag for the casket, Dependency and Indemnity Compensation Payments, potential pension payments, and educational financial aid assistance. To determine whether you qualify for any of the benefits provided, you must contact the DVA Center within the area of the country in which you reside.

If you live in the Western United States, contact:
U.S. Department of Veterans Affairs
Fort Snelling
St. Paul, MN 55111
1-800-234-5772

If you live in the Eastern United States, contact:
U.S. Department of Veterans Affairs
P.O. Box 8079
Philadelphia, PA 19101
1-800-669-8477

Organizations In Which Your Loved One Held Membership

It is important that you contact any unions, service clubs or organizations, automobile clubs, or professional groups to which your loved one belonged to determine whether you are eligible for any benefits connected with membership. Inquire about the group's life insurance policies which might have been in force at the time of death, any unused portions of annual fees or dues, and special funds or provisions which might be available for the families of deceased members. You never know what additional assistance might be available unless you ask.

Employer And/Or Business Associates

Be sure to contact your loved one's place of employment and/or his or her business associates as soon as possible. Most company employees are covered by group insurance policies. You must inquire about any benefits due you and the procedure required to file a claim. You should also ask about retirement and pension fund benefits, any accrued sick pay and vacation time which might carry monetary value, terminal pay allowances, service recognition awards, gratuity payments, unpaid commissions, disability income allowances, credit union balances, etc.

You would be wise to pay particular attention to your loved one's major medical, surgical, disability and dental coverages to determine whether you and/or your dependents are still eligible for coverage and, if so, for how long and at what cost to continue.

Mortgage Or Credit Life Insurance

Many loans, mortgages or credit cards are covered by insurance which will pay off the outstanding balance in the event of the death of the borrower. Write the company or bank in question to inform them of the death of your loved one and to ask if such insurance existed. If this coverage was in effect, you need to obtain information on how to proceed with the claim process. These companies will assist you in completing the necessary paperwork and filing the claim.

Wrongful Death Benefits

When there is a possibility that the death was the result of negligent or criminal behavior on the part of another person or a company, consult an experienced attorney immediately. It could be less stressful for you to resolve any possibilities of this nature through investigation, rather than have the unanswered questions continually clutter your thinking and feeling processes. An attorney will be able to guide you as to proper procedure for any investigations deemed necessary.

Beware — Some Cautions!

These cautions are particularly for those of you who will be receiving an inheritance or insurance settlement of some kind. The time in which you find yourself is a very delicate one. Things are not what they used to be. Sometimes there are unscrupulous people who prey upon those who are mourning the loss of a loved one. This is unfortunate, but true. If you are not careful, you can become the victim of con artists, opportunists and freeloaders. There are three areas where you can be easily victimized if you are not careful.

Obituary Chasers

If you suddenly find yourself with more money than you ever have had due to an insurance settlement or inheritance, please be aware that there are other people who "assume" that there will be a settlement in the works, as well. There are actually companies and individuals who watch the obituaries, take note of the names of survivors, look up the phone numbers, wait for one to two months (time enough for the settlement to be finalized) and then contact you with "investment opportunities of a lifetime." Unless you are aware of this practice, you might think that your funeral director or life insurance agent passed your name on to these vultures. I suggest that you place your trust in financial counselors and advisors whom you know rather than individuals who seek to offer you "incredible" deals. Again, realize that these people are out for their own gain and are very resourceful at getting what they want. Be careful!

Hasty Decisions

Sometimes, your worst enemy will not be people around you — that worst enemy will be you, yourself. There will be times when you will feel compelled, for various reasons, to make a quick decision concerning selling property, moving away, getting rid of assets, making loans to friends or family members, or buying things you really don't need. Instead, SLOW DOWN and TAKE YOUR TIME! A wise suggestion has been made concerning individuals facing the aftermath of the death of a loved one: if at all possible, make no major decisions for at least six months following the death. This is especially true where financial matters are concerned.

Freeloaders

Sometimes after the death of a loved one, you might suddenly find a great many "good friends" and favorite relatives whom you haven't seen for a long time appearing on the scene. These people will generally be supportive and want to help you make the necessary adjustments to life without your loved one. However, this is not always the case. Please try to understand that some of these people might seek to convince you to make a loan for various "necessities" that they perceive needing for themselves. You are particularly vulnerable during this time and can easily find yourself agreeing to give money away or make loans to people when you really need to be focusing on taking care of yourself. Try to make sure that you do not allow your financial situation to become general public knowledge. This is not to say that you are not free to help family members when they really need the help and you are both willing and able to agree to terms and conditions of the loan — just be sure that you do not "help yourself" into more serious problems. You are not a bank — try not to let people treat you like one!

APPENDIX B:

WRITTEN RESOURCES

The following resources may help you and/or a family member in your journey to Good Mourning.

Books — Children, Preschool To Age Eight

Bartoli, Jennifer. *Nonna*. New York: Harvey House, 1975.

Burns, Maureen, and Burns, Cara. *Life and Death in the Third Grade*. Greenville, Mich.: Empey Enterprises, 1988.

De Paola, Tomie. *Nana Upstairs and Nana Downstairs*. New York: G.P. Putnam's Sons, 1973.

Fassler, Joan. *My Grandpa Died Today*. New York: Behavioral Publications, 1971.

Harris, Audrey. *Why Did He Die?* Minneapolis: Lerner Publications, 1965.

Hogan, Bernice. *My Grandmother Died*. Nashville: Abingdon Press, 1983.

Smith, Doris. *A Taste of Blackberries*. New York: Crowell, 1978.

Stilz, Carol C. *Kirsty's Kite*. Clairmont, CA: Albatros Books, 1988.

Williams, Margery. *The Velveteen Rabbit*. Garden City, NY: Doubleday, 1971.

Zolotow, Charlotte. *My Grandson Lew*. New York: Harper, 1971.

Books — Children, Ages Eight To Eleven

Beim, Jerrold. *With Dad Alone*. New York: Harcourt, Brace, 1954.

Buscaglia, Leo. *The Fall of Freddie the Leaf*. Hew York: Holt, Rinehart and Winston, 1982.

Buck, Pearl S. *The Big Wave*. New York: John Day, 1947.

Cohen, Barbara. *Thank You, Jackie Robinson*. New York: Lothrup, Lee and Shepard, 1974.

Coutant, Helen. *First Snow*. New York: Alfred A. Knopf, 1974.

Linn, Erin. *Children Are Not Paperdolls*. Greely, Colo: Harvest Printing, 1982.

Patterson, Francine. *Koko's Kitten*. New York: Scholastic, 1985.

Richter, Elizabeth. *Losing Someone You Love*. New York: Putnam, 1986.

Whitehead, Ruth. *The Mother Tree*. New York: Seabury Press, 1971.

Books — Adolescents

Blume, Judy. *Tiger Eyes*. New York: Dell, 1981.

Brown, John M. *Morning Faces*. New York: McGraw-Hill, 1949.

Hoffman, Alice. *At Risk*. New York: G.P. Putman's Sons, 1988.

Klein, Norma. *Sunshine.* New York: Avon, 1974.

Krementz, Jill. *How It Feels When a Parent Dies.* New York: Alfred A. Knopf, 1981.

LeShan, Eda. *Learning to Say Goodbye.* New York: Macmillan, 1976.

Rudowsky, Colby. *What About Me?* New York: Watts, 1976.

Talbert, Marc. *Dead Birds Singing.* Boston: Little, Brown, 1985.

Books — Adults

Anderson, Patricia. *Affairs in Order: A Complete Resource Guide To Death And Dying.* New York: Macmillan, 1991.

DiGiulio, Robert, C. *Beyond Widowhood: From Bereavement to Emergence and Hope.* New York: The Free Press, 1989.

Grollman, Earl A. *Explaining Death to Children.* Boston: Beacon Press, 1967.

Grollman, Earl A. *Talking About Death: A Dialogue Between Parent and Child.* Boston: Beacon Press, 1990.

Lewis, C.S. *A Grief Observed.* New York: Harper & Row, 1961.

Manning, Doug. *Don't Take My Grief Away: What to Do When You Lose a Loved One.* New York: Harper & Row, 1984.

Neeld, Elizabeth H. *Seven Choices: Taking the Steps to New Life After Losing Someone You Love.* New York: Clarkson N. Potter, Inc., 1990.

Nudel, Adele R. *Starting Over: Help For Young Widows & Widowers.* New York: Dodd, Mead & Co., 1986.

Staudacher, Carol. *Beyond Grief: A Guide for Recovering from the Death of a Loved One*. Oakland, CA: New Harbinger Publications, 1987.

Staudacher, Carol. *Men & Grief*. Oakland, CA: New Harbinger Publications, 1991.

Wolfelt, Alan D. *A Child's View of Grief: A Guide for Caring Adults*. (Available from the Center for Loss and Life Transition, 3735 Broken Bow Road, Fort Collins, CO 80526)

APPENDIX C:

NATIONAL SUPPORT GROUPS

Self-Help Organizations And Support Groups

Following is a list of self-help organizations and support groups from which you may receive information concerning local chapters or groups in your area. These organizations also provide printed materials — many free of charge. Call or write to determine which group can satisfy your information needs.

AIDS Project Los Angeles
3670 Wilshire Blvd., #300
Los Angeles, CA 90010
(213) 738-8210

American Association of Suicidology
2459 South Ash Street
Denver, CO 80222
(303) 692-0985

Association for Death Education and Counseling
638 Prospect Avenue
Hartford, CT 06105
(203) 232-4825

Center for Loss and Life Transition
3735 Broken Bow Road
Fort Collins, CO 80526
(303) 226-6050

Centering Corporation
P.O. Box 3367
Omaha, NE 68103
(402) 553-1200

Compassionate Friends
(For parents whose children have died)
P.O. Box 3696
Oak Brook, IL 60522
(312) 990-0010

National Association for Uniformed Services/Society of Military Widows
5535 Hempstead Way
Springfield, VA 22151
(703) 750-1342

National Sudden Infant Death Syndrome (SIDS) Foundation
10500 Little Patuxent Parkway, Suite 420
Columbia, MD 21044
1-800-221-SIDS
(301) 964-8000 (in Maryland)

National Victim Center
307 West Seventh Street, Suite 1001
Fort Worth, TX 76102
(817) 877-3355

Parents of Murdered Children
100 East Eighth Street, B-41
Cincinnati, OH 45202
(513) 721-5683

Parents Without Partners, Inc.
8807 Colesville Road
Silver Spring, MD 20110
1-800-637-7974

The W.A.R.M. Place (What About Remembering Me?)
1510 Cooper Street
Fort Worth, TX 76104
(817) 870-2272
(Designed to provide ongoing support for grieving children,
 ages 3 to 18, and their parents.)

Widowed Persons Service
American Association of Retired Persons
1909 K Street NW
Washington, D.C. 20049
(202) 728-4370

APPENDIX D:

PERSONAL WORKSHEETS

The following worksheets can help you get started on your personal path to Good Mourning. These worksheets contain a list of potential community support resources to help you evaluate the resources which exist in your community.

You may want to write in names, phone numbers and addresses for each category listed. A telephone directory or assistance from a friend can help you develop a more complete listing of potential support.

Step One: Potential Community Support Resources

1. Your Insurance Agent/Company

_____

_____

_____

2. Investment Counselors

_____

_____

_____

3. Church/Temple/Synagogue

_____

_____

_____

4. Professional Therapists/Counselors

_____

_____

_____

5. Books/Tapes/Seminars

_____

_____

_____

6. Support Groups

_____

_____

_____

7. Legal Counsel

_____

_____

_____

8. Other Resources

_____

_____

_____

Step Two: Possible Additions to Your
Community Support System

Now, select five persons or resources from the above list to be added to your existing community support system.

1. _____

2. _____

3. _____

4. _____

5. _____

Step Three: Building Your Action Plan

From the list of five possible additions on the previous page, develop a basic, three-step action plan to determine exactly how these persons or resources will be added to your community support system. Be sure to include specific timeframes for completing each addition.

Example: I will add *a grief support group* to my community support system by *referring to Appendix C in this book to find a chapter in my area within the next two weeks.*

A. I will add _____ to my community support system by _____

_____

B. I will add _____ to my community support system by _____

_____

C. I will add _____ to my community support system by _____

_____

This progression of activities can now become your framework for creating a plan to access community support for your continued growth and recovery.